CLASSIFICATION: POETRY

A CIP catalogue record for this book is available from
the British Library.

Printed and bound in Great Britain.

Paper used in the production of books published by
United Press comes only from sustainable forests.

This South East Counties (Essex, Kent, London, Surrey &
Sussex) of England edition

ISBN 978-1-84436-744-3

First published in Great Britain in 2008 by
United Press Ltd
Admail 3735
London
EC1B 1JB
Tel: 0870 240 6190
Fax: 0870 240 6191
ISBN for complete set of volumes
978-1-84436-747-4
All Rights Reserved

www.unitedpress.co.uk

Angel's
Breath

Foreword

I firmly believe that poets are a different breed.

They are not like other people. They see and feel things with a heightened sense of awareness. They look at life in a different way.

Reading poetry is a very engaging pastime but the ability to actually *write* it is what sets poets apart from other people.

That's because poetry gives us wings. It helps us soar above and beyond the normal pathways of humanity. It elevates us to a higher plain and helps us to find new levels of existence, new realities, and new possibilities.

It's obvious to anyone reading these words that I afford poetry a kind of reverence that one would normally associate with the religious or the spiritual. That's because I believe so strongly in its power.

The effect of a poem can be like the breath of an angel. A poem can change lives for the better. It can change opinions and feelings. One poem can do so much and I sincerely hope that the collection of verses you find in these pages has a lasting and heartlifting effect on you.

Peter Quinn, Editor

Contents

The poets who have contributed to this volume are listed below, along with the relevant page upon which their work can be found.

71	Colin Dailley		Josie Turner
72	Suzanne Lemieux	105	Lindsey Marks
73	Lizzie Espinoza	106	Charlotte Llewellyn
74	Elizabeth Tittensor	107	Martine Gafney
75	Joan Rickard	108	Bosky Nair
76	Lucy Carrington	109	Hannah Rose Tristram
77	Albert Hicks	110	Marie Lambert
78	Chris Reynolds	111	Jim Bell
79	Eddie Forde	112	Patricia Dunant
80	Michael Cleere	113	Gillian Johnston
81	Lucy Stubbs		Daphne Fryer
	Thomas Smith	114	Charles Newburg
82	David Kemp	115	Patricia Jerome
83	Claire Grayson	116	Nancy Burke
84	Robert Still		David Gavin
85	Audrey Stokes	117	Natalie Clarke
	Wendy Parkes	118	Pauline Edwards
86	Anna Gruber	119	Mary Nugent
87	Gulshan Ul Amin		Janice Smith
88	Richard Freeman	120	Odette Buchanan
	Jonathon Overell	121	Derek Weeks
89	Ann Pendleton	122	Hashim Salman
90	June Lewis		Andrew Drury
91	Rebecca Hastie	123	Patricia Maynard
	Ashleigh Robyn	124	Jennifer Bourne
	Corden	125	David A Smith
92	Beata Korabiowska	126	Eileen Baldwin
93	June Lambert	127	Sharon Plumridge
94	Welch Jeyaraj	128	Diana Godden
	Balasingam		Beryl Cross
95	Bernard Tucker	129	Christine Ray
96	Vera Janczewski	130	Simon Partridge
	Sally Kemp	131	Lynn Tyler
97	Stella Redburn	132	Isabel Tepper
98	Kim Moon	133	Beverley R Stepney
	Lily Barnes	134	John Sephton
99	James Sanderson		Linda Upfold
100	Alan V Holton	135	Angela Dimond-Collins
	Raymond Blake	136	Maria Keneta
101	Valerie Luxton	137	Jane L Willis
102	Julia McDougall		Dorothy L McCuller
103	Jasmine Anthony	138	Angela Jarrett
104	Irene Chitty	139	Dominic Newman

	Dora Maxfield	172	Robert Bergin
140	Carole Ann Herbert	173	Diana Dooner
141	Diane Barham	174	Ian Tudball
142	Margaret Lawrance		Nola Small
143	Violet L Fairall	175	Sylvia Adams
	James Pyett	176	Rita White
144	Charles Wright	177	Kirsten Hogben
145	Wendy Gray	178	Kate Mackenzie
	Sheree Stringer	179	Jon Charge
146	Sheila Brown-Ellis	180	Regis O Nwofa
147	Gwen McIntyre	181	Beverley Harknett
148	Christine Collins	182	Betty Bukall
149	Matthew Dodd		Irene Bell
150	Ann Pinder	183	Clare Gill
151	Christine Kellett	184	Marion Griffin
	Muhammad Khurram	185	Roland De La Harpe
	Salim	186	Emmanuel
152	Ryoko		Faithfulman
153	Turid Houston	187	Graham Watkins
	Layka Ozkoc	188	Christopher G Elliott
154	Pearl Davis	189	Linda Carrington
155	Alan Gardner	190	Joe Creasey
156	David Chierighini		Iris Crew
157	Jacqueline Cooke	191	Valerie Fry
158	Jack Scrafton	192	Mark Shepherd
159	Alan Dickson	193	Pam Long
	Robert Duncan Martin	194	Mark Randall
160	Pat Sturgeon	195	Jo Robson
161	Sabiha Mertdogdu	196	Jessie Luckhurst
162	Sheila Bamford		Jacqueline Elson
163	Ryan Smith	197	Tracy Tabor
	Richard J Scowen	198	Robert Lane
164	Maureen Oakley	199	Martin Palin
165	Iain McGrath	200	Nikola Webb
166	Lawrence Rich	201	Charlotte Louise
	Isabella Mead		Searle
167	May McLean		Paul Jeffery
168	Margaret Ann	202	Mavis Timms
	Wheatley	203	Colin Butler
	Louise Sarah Jones	204	Tolyna Read
169	Guy Aldridge	205	Chris Renham
170	Andrew Hall	206	Hannah Phaup
171	Claire Wilson	207	Karen Cronin

208	Shirley Hannam
	Melissa McGovern
209	Valerie Helliar
210	Jessica Lempriere
211	Adham Smart
	Wayne Carr
212	Aleene Hatchard
213	Clare Nightingale
214	Angela Humphrey
215	Mary Hodgson
	Beryl Chatfield
216	Ciaran McCormick
217	Gillian Harris
	Anne M Whitington
218	Maureen Huitt
219	Rex Baker
	Nicki Watts
220	Sharon Forsdyke
221	Chane Mackay
222	Kim Sherwood

WHERE SHOULD I BE? UNDER A TREE?

By deer browsed beech, I settle down
To rest my boots on mossed-over roots
Lean right back to peer through the crown
Of golden orange and rustling brown
Beech mast prickling under my hands
I drift away through shifting sands
The buzz of insects fills my head
The sunshine warms my earthy bed
How can I rest when so much rules?
How can I not while nature calls?

Who am I, just loitering here?
Beneath blue sky such crystal clear
settle myself and breathe fine air
Under this broad tree of great age
Pleasant thoughts without any care
prompt feelings of a wise old sage
There's a lot of pleasure grounding
Deep rooted in many a way
And love for those surrounding
My ideals in every day

Bob Martin

*Dedicated to mum, dad and the family. Always let nature be
your way to understand the trials of each day.*

CHOICES

Why not take up science? The teacher said to me
You'll hold the world in the palm of your hands
If you get a PhD
In genetics or kinetics, nuclear fission or fact
Electronics or geoponics, or how hydrogen cells react
Riches will be yours, if you discover the secret of youth
Or make a fuel free car. You'll learn to seek out the truth

I thought about Hiroshima, mangled bodies in bombed Iraq
Gulf War Syndrome babies, oilfields burning,
Skies turned black,
BSE and CJD, GM foods and cloning sheep
Drugs too costly to provide though cancer victims weep

Then I thought of other things, waves surging on the sands
Village churches, silver birches, babies' clasping hands
The comfort of a mother's love, the laughter of a child
Stately beeches, bloom on peaches, bluebells growing wild
The glory of a star filled sky, equations cannot show it
Forget the scientists I thought, I'd rather be a poet

Susan Ganley

VALENTINE'S GAME

The interesting parts of my body strike lucky
And find other interesting parts of the body.
They are very hectic and happy.
Their game begins and never ends.
It is always a stalemate!

Guvench G Gench

IN HER DREAMS

She lies in terror and wonders
If the shadow will come in on his wanders
And although he was wiped from the face of the earth
His face lives on in her dreams, that are cursed
She lies there shaking in terror
And relives the eyes of the devil
He was her tormentor
And he torments still, even though he is gone
Why would she lie? The fear still goes on
She wakes numerous times in the night
And is often sweating and screaming from fright
I have to sit there, holding her hand, comforting her
Letting her know it'll be alright
And this takes up all my might
'Cause I know of the dreams
I have them too
You haunt me also
And for this you are doomed

Jade Swinerd

LOVING MEMORIES

A crisp, cold March day in Aberdeen with blue sky and
sunshine
The luxury limousine moves slowly now
So smart, solemn the driver
My beloved brother Paul coffined with lilies

Approaching the chapel white and purple crocus
Snow cascading the ground
Our car stops while the coffin is placed on dais
The minister, so composed
Kilted Eric Whyte relates stories of yesteryear
The final blessing and hymn
I trace the rainbow through the rain
Oh, love that wilt not let me go

Escorted now back to the car, emotions high
Meeting grieving friends in the cricket club
So many people who knew me as a child
Now seated in aeroplane heading to Gatwick
The stewards very professional
Remembering memories I shared with Paul
Will heal my sorrowful heart
Happy in life that shall endless be

Patricia Turpin

NEW KID ON THE BLOCK

I'm still finding out quite how it should be,
That a robin's supposed to behave.
I've been out of the nest for a week or two now,
But I'm not yet feeling too brave.

I'm what is known as a juvenile bird,
In the parlance of *birding-speak,*
Where one day I'll have brown,
I've got pale speckled down,
From my wing tips up to my beak.

I'm learning the taste of beetles and worms
And catching on quickly, moreover,
That if I perch close to a gardener at work,
I can eat what his fork has turned over.

I can cock my head sideways to listen
And my bright beady eyes will soon see,
Any signs of my hoped-for red frontage,
So that immature, doesn't mean me.

So while checking this out all you birders,
May I make myself perfectly clear,
I'll be brown, and yes, cheeky, my breast fully red,
If we meet up the same time next year.

Ann Goulder

AN ODE TO YOU

You increase the beat of my heart,
With everything you take part in.
You're like a fresh cut lawn,
On a sun drenched dawn.
You're exceptional,
And I adore you.

John Gibson

NEIGHBOURS

You never really felt alone,
Never had a digital phone,
Chatted over the garden wall,
Not like now, they are so tall.
Your kids would play from morn to tea,
Around the gardens, they felt free,
You could see from top to end,
A wave to say I'm your friend.
In troubled times, neighbours cared,
They're always there, and things you shared.
But now, you don't see anyone,
Loud music, banging doors is fun.
Kids hide in hoods outside your home,
I feel so scared and all alone.
Wish it was like before,
We never locked our back door.
You'd sit and watch the children play,
It would be lovely to do it today.

Evelyn Ingram

STORM

Heavy the sky is, and deepening and darkening,
Faint in the distance, low thunder is rumbling.
Awed by its menace, all hushed seems and hearkening,
Nearer the thunder comes, grumbling and tumbling.

Violet and vivid and forked comes the lightning,
Fierce comes the wind, as we crouch in the greenery,
Shunning the trees, for the lightning is frightening,
Deluging rain swiftly mists all the scenery.

Tumult and turmoil, the heavens seem sundering,
Nearer to Earth, hang the clouds, but our listening
Ears find relief, for more distant the thundering,
Blue in the black, and the sunlight is glistening.

Brilliant and bluer, the sky in its purity,
Sweet after storm comes the hush and the lenity,
Sweeter the air we can breathe in security,
Sweet after tumult, the peace and serenity.

Henry Harding Rogers

MUM

I spoke to you the other night
You smiled and answered me
We walked a while and talked a while
Just like it used to be
No Alzheimer's, no frailty
The years had dropped away
I wanted time to just stand still
I hoped that you could stay
But daylight dawned and you were gone
My dream had not come true
My sense of loss returned
And I'm still missing you

Rebecca Willis

Dedicated to my mum Vicki Willis who died in April. I think about her every day.

HEART'S FIRE

Hearts of silver, hearts of gold,
The story now is yet untold.
And through the desert eagle's flight,
Lighting fires in endless night.+
The world in wisdom ever turn
And in its burning shall not burn.

Charlotte Gilbert

A LIFE

She was here to see the bombs drop
She waited while the war raged and her husband was at
sea
She waited for his return from conflict, danger and terror
She was here to see his homecoming
She was at the dockside to welcome the columns of tired
men
Coming ashore, and to see his thin face smile at last
She raised their children
She buried her parents
She buried her sister and her brother
She buried her husband
She is still here, but she doesn't know why
She is waiting, but what for?
She is old
She is fragile
She smiles an empty smile, but she doesn't know why
She it still here

Jill Stearn

TREES' SEASONS

Sudden tremors, trees awoke,
As with sap uprisen
Confining buds broke
From a shuttered prison.

With primal leaves arrayed
Wound their trunks between,
As sun-sparks sprayed
Their terraces of green.

In autumn, colours stoled,
Festive banners waved.
Transmuting earth to gold,
Burnished carpet laid.

Unburdened the tree,
Winter strip blown.
Intricate anatomy
Of structure shown.

Idris Woodfield

TREES AND BIRDS

In this world of ours we need so much,
Without our trees and birds we lose touch,
Always long lasting our trees carry on,
Then our birds find shelter and food thereon.

With colour and verve our trees spread,
Always sparkling at a new day ahead,
Added by flights of birds overhead
Whatever the weather the day portrayed.

Early in spring and tree full in swing,
With many branches having to cling,
Soon comes the foliage, all gleaming,
Outshone by the colours beaming.

Meanwhile, the birds build nests,
Not for them any threat of pests,
With summer now on the days are long,
From morning to night there is song.

As days get shorter and leaves do fall,
Many birds seek shelter, big and small,
Lastly, as snow and ice begin to appear
The trees hibernate and almost disappear.

William Burkitt

THE MOUNTAINS

My heart is in the mountains,
The mountains made of stone.

The mountains have room for me and love alone.

My heart is in the mountains,
The mountains made of rock.

If you don't think you'd like it,
Please tell me to stop.

I really love them,
Those mountains, my home.

I just love them,
Those mountains alone.

Jasmine Hope Taylor

Born in Middlesex, **Jasmine Hope Taylor** has interests
including attending an art class and playing the clarinet. "I
would like to be remembered as an intelligent female and I
have written about 30 poems." Aged nine, Jasmine has an
ambition to become a famous author. "The person I would
most like to be for a day is J K Rowling because she is one
the best authors ever," added Jasmine.

ONE'S RELATIONSHIP

Ambivalent is love as it blooms and flowers,
It's a sense of colour with a summer aroma
And yet sometimes, like dying flora, it withers
For love can differ as it turns sour and bitter.
Suddenly unclear resentment does appear
Now one's confused, experiencing contempt.

As it seems one's left just paying rent
For a dissipated home, dismal and cold,
Intermittent be affection now it's absent
Replaced by scornful words and tears.
Hurtful intolerance is a clear sentiment,
It's evident romance is no longer there.

Now one's engaged in a negative gear
One's company is kept by sad despair.
But affection can briefly appear at times
Making a relationship of heart-felt strain.
So, pondering the question, why remain?
One's living in hope things will change.

Tom Mende

THE SUSSEX HILLS

Can you hear the hills a-calling?
Calling in the wind?
With arms outstretched, they bid me go,
And go I must, or die.

With their great strength, they pull me,
Pull me fast and strong,
I neither falter nor look back,
For go I must, or die.

They urge me on and on,
Across the countryside,
I cannot stop for man nor beast,
For go I must, or die.

I see them from my window,
I see them from my bed,
And to the hills I must go,
Go I must, or die.

Elizabeth Dove

PILLAR BOX

I found you standing in front of the pillar box and took pity
You cried
We went home. I did my best for you
We had fun. You smiled and laughed
I returned you to the place where you belong
You kissed my cheek and touched my hand
I closed the door

Delsie Barton-Appiah

MAYBE SHE WAS

Maybe she was a dancer,
Or was it just her name?
Maybe she was born too late?
Yet before another came,
An echo sounds the still of night,
A mother's blessing holds the light,
For one who will never see.

Perhaps she was a monster,
Sent to haunt my dreams.
To leave behind the rotting flesh,
Where lies another's screams.
Yet once again I feel it's time,
To wait another name,
So I will lay a flower
Upon her grave,
To show her I never came.

Kevin Andrews

THE OPEN DOOR

A door, an open door,
But what is the door there for?
A wall, a wall that is not joined at one end,
A wall with a door, an open door.
Behind the wall is the sea,
The sea with white cliffs.
You can see the sea through the door,
The open door.
But why is the open door in a wall that stops,
Is it that the sea is a place you once enjoyed,
A place you would like to go back to?
But what is stopping you? The door is open, the wall is not joined,
So why not go through the door, the open door?
The wall is a barrier,
A barrier to the place you once enjoyed,
A place to go and see the sea.
Go through the door, the open door
To be at the place you want to be, by the sea.

Reg Cartwright

RING THE BELLS

Ring, ring the bells
Gather all the people together
The dead are ready and waiting
Their new journeys about to begin
Brave men and women who donned uniforms
Swore allegiance to crown and country
Went wherever sent without question
Died with honour on a foreign shore
Ring, ring the bells
Hark, no-one answers, only families, widows and orphans
Who not long ago cheered and wished them God speed
Men of power who made the decisions
Hang you heads in shame at your follies
You welcomed death to your table
These are the terrible consequences
Go, ring, ring the bells
Ponder the devastating sorrows
Learn, make wiser decisions tomorrow
Awaken the country and sing praises to these heroes
Hold their memory close to each bosom
Ring the bells. Ring the bells for the dead

Joan Iveson-Iveson

BURY IT

How we liked your first exhibit,
The polished marble, flat and square
Oh, but that number two of two - shit
It doesn't seem to fit there.

According to our scatological new and myopic muse
The moral compass has gone all Pete Tong,
A bummer ... such bad news,
And it's much too long.

Like Rumplestiltskin going for gold,
Its foot seems firmly in
What with old Jack Straw all strung-out
Our collective head spins.

Yes, far too glib and big and brown.
The dialectic Ed-balls-up in the round
Negated by at least half an inch
Notwithstanding, it's rather profound.

No, no no. Let's go with the plinth.

Manus McDaid

AFTER THE STORM

In a peaceful place, calm after the storm,
Sitting firmly on land,
Quietly, I am.
Waves flowing, in and out,
Air breezing to and fro,
Gently moving along the shore.

How did it all pass? I don't know.
Where am I now? Somewhere there.
What is this being?

I am,
A single, salt-washed,
Sea-smoothed,
Speck of silken sand,
Sitting freely,
Amongst the grains.
Together,
We are the beach.

Jeanne-Michelle Lowe

Dedicated to all who have offered their encouragement and support, with special thanks to Jeremy, Anna, Christian and "The Merritts."

Jeanne-Michelle Lowe said: "I am a 43-year-old married mother of two and a student of yoga and meditation. I find inspiration in people and nature and went to London to record my poem for broadcasting on the BBC's *Stories and Rhymes*. The next time I entered a poetry competition I was again successful and my work was published. This was closely followed by obtaining sponsorship for another of my poems to be printed onto bookmarks, sales of which are helping to raise funds for Eastbourne Hospital."

THE JOURNEY

It's time to leave the office,
It's time to have some fun.
It's time to start retirement,
I wonder what will come?

Now what's around the corner?
How will I start my day?
I am about to start a journey,
Which is going to start today.

Janice Freeman

TAKE TIME TO SMELL THE ROSES

Life imposes so much stress, that it's best
to take time out to smell the roses.
Be sure this metaphor is to implore one to do
other things apart from daily work.
It is so important not to shirk at having play
time. Adults must be children too, not take the
view that play is not for them.
The mind and body work as one, and having fun
destroys the toxins in the blood.
Endorphins laugh as stress is cut, at least by half.
To take time out when one is used to being very
busy, is not at first so easy, but with effort and
endurance, eventually one sees that it's like a health
insurance.
One laughs and smiles more often, feels a sense of peace
and then before one knows it, has settled in the niche of
Taking time to smell the roses.

Mary Marriott

ODE TO SPRING

A bumblebee buzzes and flies from the hedge
A blackbird sings in the sedge,
Pink blossom scents and decks the trees
And sprouting buds form umbrellas of leaves
And the world rejoices as spring,
You are here.

The dawn chorus grows loud,
In the blue sky there's no cloud,
The mischievous cuckoo sings here then there;
Are we able to see her? No, not anywhere,
Her presence is welcome for we know spring,
You are here.

The squirrel, rabbit and playful sparring hare abound
The cows in the mead, sheep with frolicking lambs around,
In the woods there's music with a vibrant veneer
Of crocus, snowdrops and bluebell
Reminding us in this very brief spell
As the whispering wind sings,
Spring is here.

Oh spring, with what beauty you dance upon the scene
And with what grace you scatter seeds of green.

Marie Ashford

TATTOOS AND PIERCINGS MIGHT ATTRACT A QUEUE

Tattoos on bodies and graffitied walls
Reveal a youthful drive that loudly calls.
A surface urges some to make a mark,
Like children treading on fresh snow in the park.

But piercing bodies, that's another game,
Whose players feel unbroken skin is tame.
Yet piercings, like tattoos, are all agreed.
Graffiti serves just spray-can users' need.

In Rome, the early muralists were keen
To make their noble city look obscene.
In toilets, public buildings and elsewhere,
They drew and scribbled much as others swear.

Tattooists prick in colourful designs
On skin, whose owners feel such arty lines.
Will please the eyes and hearts of all who see,
By stressing looks that fine already be.

And yet do ink and metal really make
A better body, or produce a fake?
Tattoos and piercings might attract a queue,
But ravings on a wall, they spoil the view.

Allan Bula

ASPECTS OF LOVE

You are the hand that rocks the cradle,
You are the peace that comes from a smile,
You care for the lonely, the sick and the dying,
You visit the prisoner, give time to a friend.

You're faithful in good times, as well as in bad,
You speak words of kindness to those who are sad,
You wipe the brow of the one who has failed,
Whose determined efforts have nothing gained.

Cathy Mearman

THINGS

I'm being swallowed up, by
Small things, big things, tall
And short things and so much more.

No room to move,
No room to breathe
Or to do anything at all,
Even no room to stand up tall.

Eyes that follow you round the room,
The way they stand and stare
With outstretched arms
That reaches to the sky.

Small things, big things, tall
And short things and so much more,
No room at all.

Maureen A Johnston

HEART OF OAK

From an acorn I grew, I became a tree;
I stood tall and proud as an oak should be.
The woodcutters came with axes and saw;
Alas, I was a tree no more.
The bark was stripped from about my flanks;
I was cut into pieces, chunks and planks.
Fashioned and sawn then rearranged
Until my life had completely changed.
I became a table, solid and fine,
To hold and display good food and wine.
With four matching chairs I'm deemed to be old;
Almost antique, is what I've been told.
My owner, a lady, bought me second hand;
On barley twist legs I happily stand.
Serving my lady, these last thirty years,
I've witnessed great moments and splashes of tears.
Her saplings uprooted to pastures anew,
Perhaps I will follow when my time is due.
I'm treated as treasure and waxed till I glow,
A proud, old oak table, reborn long ago.

Doris Ainsworth

CATCH 22

Sitting at a bus stop, deep in thought,
The screen showed the times of the transport.
French Mum spoke sharply, to her youngster,
Who cheekily stuck, her tongue out at her.
The next bus came, stopped just ahead,
We shuffled towards this red quadruped.

Then I saw the white stick she used to feel
Led by her daughter towards the front wheel.
As the doors opened, Mama turned in the queue,
This bus, it is right, the number twenty two?
'Fraid not I replied *it's the one-o-six.*
She yelled at her daughter, *'pas cela, Beatrix.*

To me she said, *This stop, it is for my bus?*
It is, here's one, isn't that miraculous?
She thanked me, smiled, wished me *bonne journeé*
As my bus closed doors, left me, castaway
I waited for the next one, wondered about those two,
Muddled girl, blind Mama, a Catch 22.

J David Mills

OLD BANGER

She's just an old banger
That's lost all her glamour
Abandoned on a patch of turf

Her bodywork's dented
Her motion prevented
By wheelrims sunk deep in the earth

Her bonnet is busted
Her curved wings are rusted
Gone the flash coat of her birth

Once a streamlined Rover
Her mileage days over
Her condition the cruel gist of mirth

Some casually inspect her
But can't resurrect her
To restore her is more than her worth

Jessie Whitman

Born in Essex, **Jessie Whitman** has interests including
embroidery, crafts and writing. "I started writing when I
was 16, after reading my first grown-up novel," she
remarked. "My work is influenced by the work of other
authors, such as the Bronte sisters and I would describe
my style as down to earth, rustic and simple. I would like
to be remembered as a grandmother with an interesting
heirloom in literature." Aged 70, Jessie is retired with
ambitions to spend her time writing stories and sewing
quilts that tell stories as well.

SAD

Overpowering,
Overwhelming,
The sadness sets in.
Great waves of melancholy sweep over me,
A powerful deluge
Dragging me down,
Down to the depths.
Despondent bubbles burst in my head
Exploding inky blackness
Darkening every corner of my mind.
Like a whirlpool my stomach churns
Swirling me into the gloom.
A yawning deep cave draws ever nearer.
No retreat,
No chink of light.
No escape.
Unable to fight
I give in
And sink to the floor.

Jenny Mills

THE REBELLIOUS REDHEAD

Carrot top, Gingernut, I've heard them all before
Nicknames about my hair
It's really such a bore, *Ginga, ginge,* it's so unfair
Just stop these comments about my hair
If it were blonde, black or brown
There'd be no names to get me down
I'd blend right in, be one of the crowd
A head of hair of which to be proud
Mum says I'm lucky, that *red hair is cool*
And she wont let me dye it until I leave school
So I'm stuck with this hair, for at least five more years
Enduring the teasing, ignoring my peers
So I'll hold my head high, pretend not to care
Convincing myself, I'm extremely rare
And when I get older, I'll dye it jet black
A rebellious redhead, fighting right back

Kate Tuohy

Dedicated to my daughter Ellie who is the most beautiful redhead I know.

LATE SUMMER

Wheaten fields,
Azure sky,
An ancient meadow where
Wild flowers have grown.
Stored apples in the
Old black barn,
With cattle knee deep
In the algae covered pond,
And a tree swing at Addlestone.

Henry G Bradstreet

DIAMOND WEDDING ANNIVERSARY

They were childhood sweethearts
Born in Thornaby-on-Tees
Mam was in the ATS, dad went overseas
They re-kindled their love
On the bridge at Stockton-on-Tees
Then they went to Durham
For jam scones and two teas
They married in January
Knee deep in thick snow
Everyone was there, including my aunt Flo
For better for worse
Their vows they rehearsed
For richer, for poorer
In sickness and in health
Hard times as well as good have been felt
Sixty years of marriage is an achievement these days
Fingers crossed for many more wonderful years

Yvonne Husseyin

LIVING IN THE DEAD

You think you are living, when you are not,
You think you are breathing, when you actually are not,
You are just stuck in mid-air, you're
Living in the dead.

Laughter in the air,
Jokes going to and fro', flying across the room,
They are flying over your head, as you're
Living in the dead.

Maybe tomorrow,
You will finally see the light of day.
Maybe tomorrow,
You will not be alone.
Maybe tomorrow,
God will answer your prayers.

Career in tatters,
Heart broken,
Health deteriorating,
No parents, no children, no partner,
Living in the dead.

Koleta Malingamoyo

MASOCHISTIC IMPARADISE

I must wish for the dispute when I'm most masochistic
The slow, burning fury of my firing
Stops short of your face, or heart
But it's a glad sight when the veins do burst
And cry blue murder from artery to artery
Each pore filled with red

Watching even your voice choke within itself
As the lumbering begins from coast to coast
And the easiness of gain and the hardship of loss
If only God had blessed all with the gift of her trust

It's all masochistic, the pleasure from pain
Like war for our freedom, our freedom for chains
If murder is achievement, this is not an earth
I declare myself alien, from a separate universe

I do not wish to greet God, in her grace and disdain
To say I am your human, who pleasured from pain

Leila Badawi

A FALLING LEAF

Falling gently down and down
Softly, floating round and round
When suddenly without a care
Up it springs into the air
Tossing, turning, up it goes
Dancing there, prancing here
Turning swirling, to and fro
Then down it dives towards the moss
Without a sound it lands so soft.

Patricia Flood

JACK-IN-THE-BOX

That was in the old days-
Now it's 'H' in the tunnel,

Popping up three times-
No more energy

For deep breaths!
Cramp in the arms!!

Too long inside,
Wanting fresh air!!!

And the patient
Administrator

Of the tunnel scan
Sighs!

Hannah Hobsbaum

I AM

I am Captivus,
The angel that says, *The man asleep in war is left hungry in peace,*
I am the dream-caster of decapitated heads.

I was the dog lost in space by himself,
And saw Neptune watching in the blackness.
The glittered asteroids said,
The planets move silently above your head, making futures with an exhale.

And I am the only one he obeys,
Sputnik to the infinite races hiding behind the stretch of stars.
I am Captivus, the last of the minotaurs,
I inhaled the blood of Mars, I am the face of you.

I smell the dying gods under my fingernails as I build our war,
The guardians of the earlier races extinguished.
Now you are alone with me
And you will hear nothing but our echoes in the bleeding space.

Sara Badawi

NATASHA IN THE GRAVE

So much economy and not even a word of praise.
I dredged up gallons of misery from the well of her disdain,
She loved my gentle patter, even as she hated my casual
acceptance of pain.

Life is for the beautiful, like you baby,
I told her, *You will always reign.*
Lesser mortals like myself have got to make a real effort
If we are ever to attain.

Attain what? A niche, a comfortable spot in the shade,
A chance to feel wanted as
We combine our best intentions with
A voice that trembles in the rain.

The silence of her death leaves me craving for a dream
As I crumble in empty space
Clutching a notion of togetherness
Which shall never be regained.

Carlos Nogueiras

44

SPLASH

Silver smooth and gentle ease,
A world adapting to every need,
Like ancient silk caressing
A gentle ripple in the mercury,
The only sign of her progression.

All weightless, suspended in a force,
Yielding, giving with gentle restraint.
Light leads a dance of tiny sparkles
And in their midst, she felt ethereal,
A timeless aeon's worth of oneness.

With a splash of deodorised armpits,
The aqua-group arrived,
Flailing through the calm,
Fragmenting her quest
In chloride dissolution.

She reached for the coldness of the ladder,
Curving in on itself in silent surrender,
Still seeking absolution.

Veronika Marsh

THANK YOU FOR THE GIFT OF FRIENDS

For friends are there for you
Ready to share your pain and joy
Interested in what you say and do
Excepting you for who you are
Never judging you right or wrong
Deep within your heart they stay
So show them how you love them today

For what I say must be true
Because I have found a forever friend in you

Pauline Kirby

RETURN JOURNEY

I travel by plane, train or car,
To see wonders near and far.
But wherever I may roam,
I am always glad to be coming home.
Flying back, I see below me,
A patchwork quilt that is my country.
Fields of light green, fields of dark green,
Wherever I've been I will not have seen.
A sight more rare,
Nor a country more fair.

Barbara Cleere

BRITAIN

The tube spills out its load of people
From all nations
Kind compassionate Britain
The NHS and its patients

Busker's songs, new and old
Where are the streets paved with gold?
Young and old, black and white
In a hurry, seeking light

There's no time to stop and stare
Someone dies, does anyone care?
Everyone's striving to do what they can
To earn money, survive, with some sense of calm

Despite the pressure it's a great place to be
There's talent galore for the world to see
Britain is still standing tall and proud
It's good to be just one of the crowd

Patsy Harrington

SUPER SONNET

Amid the car park and the hustle and bustle,
Though it be winter, the season of yule,
The wind whipped up a phantom rustle,
An eerie echo of leaves autumnal.
For outside the heaving superstore,
Trees were planted for reasons aesthetic,
As consumers came back for more and more,
Feeding needs which were materialistic.
Their apathy taking so much for granted,
A by-product of a post-modern age.
Never noticing trees that were planted,
Now adorned with their pseudo-foliage.
For entwined within the trees skeletal bower,
Were many and many a bag of plastic,
Discarded by hands whose standards dropped lower,
A beckoning future ever so drastic.

Long gone were the bird's sweet tunes,
Replaced by miserable black exhaust fumes.
Artificial leaves, now blowing in the wind,
From this scene can we ever rescind?

Steve Hancock

ODYSSEY

The river runs to the end of its time
Mid the sepals of matching unity
On flower-capped vines and dark green leaves.
And glimpses of light between the trees,
Give hope of chances
And glances of laughter
Irretrievably trapped in a time gone by
Or a possible future.

And round the corner, Uncle Joe's Diner,
With its blaring sound
And its garish light,
Is the source of earthly nourishment
Until the croaking of frogs in the morning
Leads back to the river
And on to the sea,
To inseparable unity with the ocean.

Elizabeth Ward

WAITING FOR THE WIND

It's like waiting for the wind,
Does it blow gently, does it blow strong
Or does it even blow at all?
Maybe it's settled for a quieter life,
Maybe it's joined the rainfall,
Tremors of earth and the hot, blazing sun
Cannot control the wind
For the wind is a creature who never
Gives in.
Its mystery never unfolds.

Janet C Thompson

SEASONS

The instant sap of springtime,
Its instinct keen and certain,
Explodes in tree and hedgerow,
Flings off the winter curtain.
The dance that drives it dizzy,
Was driven from the earth
By nature's blind commandments,
Insistent on re-birth.

The stubborn plants of autumn,
So bent on bare survival,
Anticipate harsh winters,
Expect no strong revival.
They store their careful moisture
Against assault and treason,
And nurture stern resources
To endure another season.

Tim Bleach

MY CHOO HEAVEN

I will make my mark upon the parquet floors of this world
In these stiletto heels, teetering forward, bottom in the air

I will pad through life in pink flats
Stretching hamstrings and minds as I go

I will gallop through my life in black satin mules
With my hair trailing in the wind

In my blue-spotted wellies I will charge
Through the rain-soaked London, jungle of the night

And I will dance joyously through my life
In silver trainers, made just for the disco

And when, finally, I put my best feet forward
To meet their designer
I will show them clad in callouses and corns and he will know that
I moved well-shod through this world

Judith Perry

VERSE

Why don't verses rhyme these days?
It's something I cannot fathom.
School days were fun
When you could see,
Line one would rhyme with three.

Why don't poems have to rhyme
At least occasionally?
It's so hard to learn,
Unless you're sure,
That line two will rhyme with four.

If poems rhymed just a little bit,
Then foolish folk like me
Would read the verse
And feel like heaven,
If line five would rhyme with seven.

But verses come well thought out
And by illustrious poets,
I explore new work
But in vain I wait
For line seven to rhyme with eight.

Billie Filler

IF

If I were rich, a car I would buy,
Around the world I'd sail or fly.
No need to earn money, no need to try.
With a flourish I'd sign, this name or mine,
To a cheque, without wherefore or why.

But, where would the pleasure be for me,
With cash to be spent on endless spree.
Then I'd die and leave it to charity,
If I were rich.

Elizabeth Crumlish

MY LOVE AND I

I am a country girl. Money, I have none
But I have silver in the stars
And gold in the morning sun
The winds ripple the long wheat and the hanging rye
Next to my love I am
Together in the barley fields we lie

Riches, I may never own, but rich in love I be
Kisses are given
As he rests close to me
Gazing upon you, he who I long
Being my only wonder
Making this heart of mine beat strong

I am a country girl. Money, I have none
But as long as you live in my life
The greatest prize I have won

Gemma Davis

THE PEARL

Our anniversary, yes, thirty years, our pearl,
Soon the grand celebrations, will unfurl.
We might fly around the country in a plane,
Or, maybe a long weekend to sunny Spain,
The Bahamas sounds rather inviting to me,
A posh hotel, yummie food, by the sea.
Perhaps hire a camper van, well, he might,
And sleep under the stars, for the night,
Never thought camping was on the agenda,
Would like to do something we'd always remember.
We will probably just get up and go,
What about Paris? That's only a stone's throw.
I will have to wait, until the anniversary eve,
To see what surprise is up his sleeve.
Of course, we could always just stay at home,
So then he can paint the garden gnome.
Our pearl anniversary, we'll celebrate in style,
Like our life together, many a giggle and smile.
I wonder what our special celebration will be,
Expect we're out for lunch and home by tea.

Jenny Williams

THE WEDDING

We've been invited to a wedding
That's why we're standing here
Surrounded by great mounds of food
And spirits, wine and beer

The guests have travelled near and far
From north, south, west and east
To celebrate this happy day
And partake of the feast

Old friends embrace with hugs and smiles
It's been so long, we know
Since such a gathering as this
Took place a while ago

We all look somewhat older
Thicker waists and more grey hairs
Too stiff to stand around too long
We quickly bag the chairs

Though compared to the bride and groom
We're relatively young
For the bride is eighty-seven
And the groom is ninety one

Angela Stanford

THE LITTLE THINGS IN THE LOFT

It's the little things that we remember
When looking back upon our life.
The first tender kiss as sweethearts
Then the joy of being your wife.
Here's a picture from our wedding
Feast in the hotel room that faced the east.
The candied fruit and the orange half peeled
And the flagon of wine that somehow got spilled.
Look at the photos that we both took
And we stuck them in that old book.
The post cards we collected have been neglected.
Here are the shoes so tiny and neat
They sat so prettily on our first born's feet.
Can you believe he is now fifty two?
And putting his foot in a size twelve shoe.
These little things are worth much more than gold
They are our lifetime story
That will always be told.

Shirley Wescombe

*Dedicated to my late husband. For Lawrie; my life, my joy,
my darling boy.*

Born in Sutton, **Shirley Wescombe** has interests including
walking and listening to opera. "I started writing a year ago
after joining a poetry group. We are encouraged to have a
try," she explained. "My work is influenced by writers such
as Wordsworth and Pam Ayres and I would describe my
style as rhyming couplets and topical. I would like to be
remembered as a rounded human being." Aged 73, Shirley
is retired with an ambition to stay healthy and to live life to
the full. "The person I would most like to meet is Pam
Ayres because her versatility and sense of humour inspire
me," added Shirley.

MY BEST MATE

When you were young, just thoughts of play
On summer days in backyard hay
And welcomed all who came to stay

In winter, you were just the same
So full of life and friendly game
In muddy water you would swim
Causing all to raise a din

As years passed by, you changed so little
Your creamy hair so full of colour
You walked with little huff
And perhaps, just then and there, a puff

And yet throughout your long life through
The puppy play remained so true
No thought of anger or aggression
You taught us humans all a lesson

In this sad heart, those lessons taught
Alas, I will always be fraught
But in this heart, a special place for those memories
Of my special mate

Bob Weller

THE LANCASHIRE CONNECTION

A tingle in your cheeks and cold wet feet
The sharp wind hinders if the hill gets steep
Now you hear the water as you catch your breath and stop
Through the close knit pine trees to the vast moorland top

They say that on a clear day
You can see for miles around
And apart from nature's voices you will never hear a sound
Contours of the world you see when looking from this
height
The chequered shades of brown to green
Meet the sky as all the trees would like

That big farmhouse where the family once lived
Stands alone in the ruins now the family has moved
They left for the noisy city many years ago
Leaving it to rot above an ageing village below

Back down the hill to the village inn light
Which looks huge as evening gives way to night
In fact, it's quite small with low beams from the ceiling
Like home by the fire, a beer and good reading

Peter Diprose

MOANING MONOLOGUE

Riding slowly on this bus,
Wishing I didn't have to, but I must.
Going to a place where imagination is spare,
Where darkness rises in its lair.

An unhappy time, an unhappy place,
Where the minuscule working space,
Leaves us, the humans, angry and trapped,
Even monkeys know better than that.
To avoid the cages of human hand,
What we, ourselves, have reduced to man.

Daniella Dörfler

MOONLIT

Moonbeams shuttered by scudding clouds
Break through, picking out night-time movements,
Within the stillness of sullen nocturnal hours.
Silent on the heavy air floats, the watchful owl.
As if petrified, mouse and vole stay, the owl glides by,
And vole and mouse continue their moonlit search.
On dewy leaves slugs and snails make feasts,
Celebrating the sleep of thrush and crow,
Unaware of the scurrying hedge pig or snuffling brock;
Tonight they celebrate still before sliding to rest by dawn.
The pace and peace of night,
The roaming or rest in the moonlight
Mark the being in creation's own appointed time,
When day and night, dark and light
Are separated by the sun's rise or fall,
Made fools of in a lunatic rhythm
As the moon's smiling face may wax or wane.

Paul Cox

CHILD OF TIME

Sometime, I feel like a little child
Tumble rough, a little wild
With wind and rain upon my hair
I skip and run, I know not where

But oh, to stay a little child
With innocence of life, so mild
A thing. 'Tis not to be
For I need adult company

Although full grown, I could be wild
Possessing thoughts just like a child
Loving and laughing, feeling free
But where's my love, oh where is he?

Time is but a precious thing
Flies like a bird upon the wing
So flying, come my love to me
The only thought I have. 'Tis thee

Isabel Eakins

GHOST

I went to Paris to kill the ghost.
He'd relocated there
finding the environs of Paris
so much more conducive
to his wispy ways
than those of Leeds.
But the bugger kept nipping back
to remind me.
Then he'd do that fading trick
to re-appear, so he said, in Fauchon's,
where they do the best
rose-petal tea in the world.
So I went to Fauchon's
and sipped rose-petal tea
willing him to join me
for a final reckoning.
Then I entwined the elusive enchanter
round my little finger
and left him in the remains
of my rose-petal tea.

Olivia Newbery

THE PRICE OF FREEDOM

Three brave and fearless, eager lads, at eighteen years a
soldier,
To free a land from tyranny, before they are much older.
A bullet strikes the beating heart of soldier number one,
He smiles no more, he played his part, his short life's work
is done.
Pounding guns, exploding shells maim soldier number two,
No more to hear his sweetheart's voice, enjoy an English
view.
A deftly hidden booby-trap does for soldier three,
He suffers loss of arm and legs to set some strangers free.

Two brave and bitter soldier lads, accompanied by a coffin,
Return home to their loved ones, battles best forgotten.
Inspiration punished by the sights that they have seen,
But, rewarded by a medal and a handshake from the
Queen.

At eighteen years a soldier, disillusioned, now they shout,
We gave our all, our comrade too - is this what life's about?

Toni Leighton

SONNET

Had Hitler died an obscure youth?
his epitaph had been the truth.
For how can mourners for the infant dead,
envisage how they might have lived instead?
Perish in youth like Little Nell,
no question of your going to hell.

Imagine little Myra killed,
with all that promise unfulfilled,
and all the Hindley clan bereft,
the waste of it, her whole life left
Before her. See her youthful face
beam innocence from every tabloid place.

The good die young, it's understood.
Accumulating sins takes time.
Scant opportunity for crime.
It's simply that the young die good.

Penny Solomons

Penny Solomons said: "I live in North London with my husband Laurence. I leaned to write at the age of five and have not stopped since, mostly journals, letters, short stories, restaurant reviews and poetry. I have published a book, *The Urban Guesthouse,* and several poems. An important influence has been my father's letters, written to my mother between 1943 and 1946 when he died of tuberculosis, aged 30. My ambition is a 21 inch waist, my worst nightmare is Jeremy Clarkson and world peace is my biggest fantasy. I perform my poetry in various modest, yet disreputable London venues."

A TIME FOR CELEBRATION

So you've got where you intended
Multi-skilled Mercedes man
Your long quest was swiftly ended
Just as in your devious plan.

Restaurant meals and concert going
Theatre visits duly led.
Like trips to see the flowers growing,
Just as you had hoped, to bed.

Thirty pounds was all it needed -
Silver has gone out of fashion -
Loyalty at once receded.
Thanks to lies and her compassion.

Infidelity's addictive
Flaunt your triumph while you can,
'Til she finds your life restrictive
And seeks out some other man.

Norman Longmate

THE DAWN

The sunlight in my life,
A new page in life,
So please ignore so far-away distant yesterdays
So peace can be found.
Birds singing, let's hail their message,
Enter your life so very new in their lives,
For bird song is the sunlight of our lives,
For beauty can soar of fly,
Trees their haven,
Finally their song,
Our heaven.

Raymond Jones

LOVE LIES CRUCIFIED

Love lies will crucify you
Lying for love will crucify the love in you
Love will lay down its life for you
Love will lay down with you, love will lie for you
Love will lie to you, you will crucify yourself for love
You crucify love for yourself
Why does love lie crucified, on a bed of nails sacrificed?
The altar of your desire, the redemption of higher fire
A tower of strength, the tree of knowledge
A honeyed kiss and sweet breath, the wisdom of experience
The denial of love will lay in you
The love lie will nail you too
Why do we always hurt the one we love
With the acid tongue of love undone?
Must love always lie crucified, before we can reach
paradise?
Must love always lay sacrificed, before love lies glorified?

Keith Martin

SOUTHWARK CATHEDRAL

Over the water from old London city
Built by the river centuries ago
Southwark cathedral, tracing medieval history
Flies a bright flag from its graceful square tower
From London Bridge, go down the dank steps
To the churchyard garden laid out below
To the sun-lit lawn and shady trees
Where workers, tourists and beggars find peace
Hemmed in by new buildings, accessed by alleys
Overhead trains on elevated rails rattle and rumble by all
day

Inside are lofty gothic arches
Candles flicker in a hallowed space
Housing precious objects and effigies
Once martyrs were condemned here for heresy
Once Shakespeare drew crowds to his plays nearby
London Bridge paraded heads on spikes
Bear-baiting was rife, people were poor
And Bankside was a den of vice

Now, only the echo of footsteps and whisper of voices with-
in
And the rising harmonies of the choir as evensong begins

Rachel Smith

IF YOU HAVE MEASURE OF TIME

If you have measure of time,
You just might find that you and your friends
Will be remembered as an able tribe.
You may complete some epic journey together,
Or even resurrect values others left behind.
Though some remain married or tied to their work,
A band of gold, binds them still to weather-beaten idols,
Where the chief among you first struck his cobalt design.
The rest gathered like disciples in a bar,
As posterity remarks upon you,
That true measure of time.

Eddie Saint Jean

FACE VALUES

Lord, why do I treat my neighbours badly
And judge them so unfairly?
Like a pack of cards, I put them into suits
Yet you alone know the exact state of their hearts

Lord, why do I distinguish black from white?
For the bible says all are precious in your sight
In Heaven, the greatest shall be least of all
Poor men on earth may, in front of you, stand tall

Lord, why do I look up at kings and queens
And then look down on those I call has-beens?
For as you walked the earth, you gave value
To servants I place behind me in the queue

The answers to these questions lie within
We see others in pure light upon confession of our sin

Paul Bebbington

CALL OF THE SEA

I stand alone on soft, white sand
A sense of desolation takes me by the hand
Oceans of gentle clouds drift in the air
And you are here and everywhere

I can feel the calling of the sea
Enchanting, still and full of mystery
It seems to whisper your name
I know it will never be the same

A gentle breeze caresses my hair
It is then I feel my heart lies bare
Why did you have to leave so soon?
You are allusive still, just like the moon

I step lonely into the gentle swell
Just where our footsteps last fell
Why did you let me go free?
It is only together we should be

Light winds blow and toss the sea
Will they bring you back to me?
Or when I feel this sudden pain
Will it extinguish all and end this flame?

Barbara Leswell

SET ME FREE

How drowsily the day starts, soft and fawning
No clatter and buzz of alarm clocks
But birdsong winging its way from the distant woods
Calling me up out of the restless world of dreams
The real world awaits my presence
Trains and cars and office desks
The casual looks from colleagues in suits
How bleak our lives, in this man-made hell
The phone rings; no, I'm not here
I'm with the birds in the distant wood
Listening to the leaves unfolding
The soft feel of flowers brushing my fingers
Why is my body here in front of this computer?
Looking at spreadsheets, meaningless figures
Important to the boss, a tangle of numbers
Trapping me in useless bonds
Set me free to roam the woods and fields
Where I can breathe unsullied air
But here I must stay to earn my crust
Until my body turns to dust

Jean Staveley

SYSTEM FAILURE

I came to download my thoughts
But my friend, you were not well
You caught a chill, flu even
And with a sneeze, you became disconnected

Your memory severed from the phone
No conversation could you enjoy alone
And I also was left in the cold
Friendless and homeless in that

My thoughts stayed with me
And couldn't be converted
From a beautiful font into print
And thereafter bound into a book

These thoughts
May have forever stayed unformed
In fact, some might say they
Definitely still are

But I persevered in my conversations
Next, I will try new routes and topics
I will search new ports and pamphlets
And in future, I will try to understand you better

Barbara Tozer

COUNTRY PLEASURES

Ah, a pleasant walk in the countryside
You need no A to Z or pocket guide
Just wander here and there, where you will
And listen to the bird song until
You come across a deer or two grazing
And it is then that you begin raising
Your expectations of a pleasant time
Far away from the city grime

The sun shines and the leaves flutter
The flowers glow the colour of butter
But something constantly assails the senses
As you traipse along and straddle the fences
Is it cow? Is it pigs? What is that smell?
Ooh, all of a sudden, I feel quite unwell
All this beauty of things I'm among
Damn it, I think I just trod in some dung
Just when I thought it was all so pretty
Sod it, I think I prefer the city.

Colin Dailley

Colin Dailley said: "I have been writing on and off for 20 years. I started by writing diaries and then poetry, about 15 years ago. Since then I have written short stories and I am working on a novel. I get my inspiration from reading other prose writers and poets, and my own reflections on life. I should like to be remembered as a writer of poetry and prose. I love travel and would like to do some travel writing. I believe very much that whatever you do in life, a sense of humour is essential."

ROAD KILL

Poor Mr Badger.
Aheap in dirt and gravel,
Slumping where tarmac gives way
to flattened verge,
The passing place for vehicles' dance
in the rushing hours.
Your contours seep
as the days move on,
Your powdered bones
become a dust within the parcel
of your parchment skin.
Your fur clinging on
so that, in your paper state,
we may still know it's you.
No gentle decomposing
in a leafy bower
but mummified
by the daily pounding
of a thousand wheels.

Suzanne Lemieux

THE STARS ARE CRYING

The stars are crying
Flashes of sparkle in the dark
I want to know
Their forms, their mystery.

In the silence, someone could be crying
I cannot hear them.

Your smile, a light
I think about your warmth
The fire in your soul,
You and me floating into space
Through the universe.

But tonight the stars are crying
I can hear them, but I can't see you.

Tonight the stars are crying
Vast spaces of emptiness between us
I wish they would get smaller
Instead space expands
And only the sound of
The stars crying fills that place.

Lizzie Espinoza

THE ROMANTIC RIVER IN LITERARY RICHMOND

The romantic river flows through literary Richmond
As the Thames in London sets the scene
And the bridge is built across the rippling water
Where the riverbanks run along the pathway
While visitors walk in meadow nursery lands
Clasped hands held in a memorable, modern epoch
A fashionable town on the theatre stage
Contemporary architecture adorns the cityscape
The vista of the park on the hill
And a royal palace stands resplendent
Heritage and history in centennial triumph
Turners painting in a pictorial view
Art is illustrated in museum galleries
Princes and patrons donate to the nation
A place in England's capital garden
From stream to placid island ait
Courting couples stroll by the wayside
Where feelings flourish in the summer sun
And flowers fill the scent of the season
Love is the time in the heart of happiness

Elizabeth Tittensor

SUCCESS

This paper resting on my lap
It's really set a cursed trap
I've racked my brains, I'm going mad
I really shouldn't be so sad.

With furrowed brow, I tore my hair
The answer was I knew not where
I bit my lip, gnashed my teeth
Stared at the thing in disbelief.

With reference books around me strewn
I studied them with mounting gloom
An answer here, a strange new word
The meaning of which I've never heard.

But slowly and surely it all came clear
I glanced at the clock, midnight was near
The smile of victory crossed my face
I was no longer in disgrace.

I can now look the whole world in the eye
And say without a word of lie
Across and down I've filled the lines
I've solved the crossword in The Times!

Joan Rickard

STARVING

Like lustrous pearls, your words of wisdom shone bright
On this cold, indifferent world, to make many realise
That the efforts of head did not suffice
But had to co-ordinate those of heart

How right you were to emphasise
That food of love, though vital for life,
Was in short supply for everyone!

As lessons of compassion, your actions louder than words
Not only fed souls starved of affection and love
But had power to transform today's world
Into a happier tomorrow for all!

So everyone has to concede that your big heart
Full of warmth and bursting with love
Made all nations fall at your feet
To let you, *Queen Diana* of Compassion and Love
Reign until the end of time, just to remind
each and everyone what our mission is in life

Lucy Carrington

THE STREAM

From birth flowing from green grasses
Like silver thread lights as it passes
Spreading out fingers on slopes of green
Bouncing on stones to broaden the scene
The trickle is now becoming a flow
As rain clouds descend to help make it grow
Flowing now steadily it reaches a base
And slowly meanders not running a race
The stream now winding its way is led
Through troughs and hollows it makes its bed
Through fields and copse and marshy ground
It gains new life from all around
Birds, insects, small mammals too
Wild flowers from its moisture now grew
Flowing freely now, it widens and grows
From trickle to brook to stream it flows

Albert Hicks

HER SON CAME HOME

In her sadness and his glory
She held her head up high
Now was not the time to grieve
Tonight, alone, she'll cry

Silence, then with rifles aimed
They fire into an empty sky
The last salute to this brave soldier
No, this was not the time to cry

All this time, her head is screaming
He's not your soldier, he's my son
All your words won't bring me comfort
How many must die until your war is won?

She struggles to understand the reason
Why we have to kill our own
Life's too precious to spend fighting
And this is how our boys come home

She prays one day we won't need conflict
To stop the few of power and greed
And man will spend more time just living
And pain and suffering will recede

Chris Reynolds

AREN'T WE LUCKY TO LIVE HERE

Across from the Green Man, where the sheep
Pen stands empty, is a new seat dedicated to
Harry, a war hero, who loved the Common
Not that he hardly ever ventured out onto it
He liked looking out from the pub
With a pint, as I am doing now
I can see a ranger clad in brown
Ride away from the tea and paper stalls
By the commemoration bench inscribed
Aren't we lucky to live here?
Under which this once young sergeant's ashes rest
Normally, we are too busy and preoccupied to be
Appreciative of our surroundings
But exceptional people who have been through
So much and done so much for others
Know the importance of contentment, simplicity and time
Now, when I visit the hostelry, I often dwell
Upon his words as I try to cope with the
Wind-up merchants who wouldn't be here but for the likes
Of Harry, and his overwhelming generosity of spirit

Eddie Forde

THE LEAF GATHERER

Hollywood called in younger days and made a star of you
A famous face on cine screens in tinsel town's who's who
Movie days over, you retire to your ranch
A multitude of sunsets to view
But after some years, they all lose their glow
Time to start life anew

California the place, and politics the game
Placards and banners bear that movie star name
Summits with Thatcher, Gorbachev and Zhao
Finger on the button, the most powerful and how

The years take their toll and the mind once so bright
Now plagued by dementia and Alzheimer's dark light
Hands once on the button now grasp a pool net
Gathering leaves from the water before they sink low
Back turned from the pool, making a leaf pile
Bodyguards throw more in, then turn, wink and smile

Rest now, old cowboy, your race is run
Hopefully at peace on that nirvana shore
The leaf gatherer is no more
Goodbye, Mr President

Michael Cleere

NEW-BORN JOY

To freeze-frame forever in my heart
Those moments of mutual tenderness
When you respond with a smile
To my look of gentle care.
When your little frame shakes with chuckles
Delighting in your new-found sound
When lying there, you kick your legs so joyfully in the air
Or clasp tightly my fingers in your hand.
When morning comes and you first perceive me
And reward me with such a look of joy
And cavernous ear-to-ear smiles.

Lucy Stubbs

HIDE AND SEEK

I counted to one hundred
For the hundredth time this year
Don't leave the road
We were warned

I can't find you
Behind the car we hit with the ball
Behind the vacant garage
Behind the yellow smelling tree
Don't leave the road
We were warned

I'm twenty-six now
Twelve long summers have passed
I stopped seeking because your
Face disappeared
If you're still hiding
You win

Thomas Smith

WINTER ON SEA

The crashing waves, just out of reach,
The sullen sand, upon the beach.
The shadow of a deserted pier,
Not a holiday treat, now winter's here.

No ice cream cones, no children's rides,
Just bold aggressive change of tides.
No candy floss, no family smiles,
Just a promenade that's closed for miles.

No coach arrivals, or one day trips,
No cockles, winkles, fish and chips,
Boarding houses closed up tight,
No coloured lights displayed at night.

No boating trips, cream teas no more.
This is winter down by the shore.
Just empty trains and vacant streets,
It coldly shivers, till summer heats.

David Kemp

BLACK CLOTHES

Why am I wearing black?
Am I mourning the family I had,
For the madness I never had,
But not allowing myself?

For the loss of love in the world,
For the fullest love I've known that
I've destroyed.

I'm mourning over the minds that think
Like machines and have created the machines
In their own image.

I am mourning about the light years of stars
And galaxies from the world, because I can't find them,
All in one place, which is my heart.

But above all I'm mourning about my own life,
Maybe I may be a being that may just be.

Claire Grayson

MR CLUMSY

It must be the way I get out of bed
I always seem to land on my head
By this time, it's taken me an hour
Sort myself out and have a shower

Finally get myself dressed
Now, I look like a complete mess
I'm already half an hour late
I'm getting into a right flustered state
Worrying about that all important date

Get pulled up by police, what can I say?
It just hasn't been my lucky day
First, they test my eyes and then I was breathalised
Stopped for a chat, my back tyre went flat
Finally, get in the car and drive away
My journey has now taken me half the day
Nothing seem to be going my way

I'm driving along, something's rattling about
Could it be the engine falling out?
I wonder what else is in store
Or who may come knocking at my door?

Robert Still

IMAGINATION

Take a silken strand of starlight,
Mix with a moonbeam or two.
This is the stuff of which dreams are made of,
Let your imagination take flight,
As you contemplate the morning dew
The beauty all around you, so often goes unseen,
But nature always rules supreme.
Forget your cares, for just an instant,
Lift up your eyes, and let your heart soar free,
Towards the heavens, ever constant
And give thanks for everything you see.

Audrey Stokes

CAROL SINGERS

They came a-knocking late one night
Carol singers at my door
Stood huddled together
In the terrible weather
Their voices angelic and pure
One held a candle
One had a lamp
As they sang Merry Christmas
In the cold and the damp

Their faces were lit by the front porch light
Their smiles were sweet and their eyes were bright
As they stood in the doorway
Their faces aglow
The night air fell silent
And it started to snow

Wendy Parkes

DARTMOOR

Peace, quietness, space
Crystal clear springs, air so pure
Old and new life
Side by side on the moor
Grazing ponies, green meadows
Awesome stone circles
Towering menhirs, moving shadows.
Ancient woodlands
Carpets of bluebells in spring
Butterflies, birds, heathland ablaze with ling

Walking hand in hand
Over granite boulders, dainty flowers
Exploring vast open land
Climbing hills, remote Tors
Exhilarating views across the moors,
Close to eternity, secure
Defying injury by men and time
Dartmoor's beauty will remain

Anna Gruber

ASIAN BRIDE

Dresses glittering,
Bangles jingling,
Noise and laughter,
Food and drink.
Smell of flowered
And perfume,
A decorated room,
An adorned bed.
And on the bed,
Lay a bundle of red.

The bundle moved,
It raised its bowed head.
In it's eyes
Hundred stories,
Untold,
Shimmered,
Glimmered,
How did it reach there,
From someone, from somewhere,
Did someone ask this bundle
Did it want to be here?

Gulshan Ul Amin

TROUBLES

Everyone has it, once in their life,
In which they experience a trouble or strife.
Well, I'm here to tell you, despite through it all,
The order you face may not be so tall.
For I'm here to help you through those once in a whiles,
And help you surpass all life's little trials.

And when you believe that life can't go on,
That is the time when you must be strong.
As you'll always have someone in which to confide,
When you've been through it all, you've laughed and you've
cried.

Richard Freeman

CHRISTMAS MORNING

The woods, it seems,
Have woken to a sombre Christmas day, with
Old-man's beard, sparse berries and green catkins,
The sum of their display.

But though there is no carolling, the birds
Defer to silence, don't sigh,
For songs last summer heard them sing.
And though there's no carousing, the air
Is stone cold sober, don't dream,
Of how you'll slake your thirst with spring.

For looking back or forward is to overlook what's here;
These meagre-seeming tokens make full celebration,
Set seed and ready fruit and pollen forming,
Blazon the past, the now and even incarnation.

Jonathon Overell

MISTY

Your picture hangs upon my wall,
Up there in pride of place,
A springer spaniel to the life,
You gaze upon my face.

You were born when I was young,
But in fact, we never met.
You lived your life and played your games
As someone else's pet.

Oh, how I wish I'd known you,
Had felt your silky fur
And watched you run and jump for joy,
Guard your ball and never stir.

Your eyes intense and soulful,
Soft mouth, a curving smile.
I always feel I know you
As you watch me all the while.

Ann Pendleton

YOU LEFT ME

You went out of the door
No backward glance,
No partner for life,
No partner to dance.
You said you loved me
With all your heart and mind,
How could you do this to me my love,
When you'd always been so kind?
No hint, I had no suspicion,
You played it with secrecy,
Until that day, I had no idea
You would be leaving me.
I hated you, yes, hated you,
Then someone did explain,
You wanted to hide the fact from me,
That you were in great pain.
As time went by and my mind cleared,
You were not to blame I realised,
You had tried so hard not to hurt me
But you had to leave me - because you died.

June Lewis

SOMETHING

Something abstract and inconsequential,
Something wild, magnificent and wonderful.
A piece of the picture, a fragment of the puzzle.
A disconcerting look from high above,
Down a long nose and hateful eyes.

Something about the sun.
Something connective and overdone.
A point of no escape, a feeling,
Of endless guilt.
A triumphant stare, into the sands,
Of desert ahead.

Rebecca Hastie

LOOKING DOWN DEEP

Do people notice people's hearts, or just the shape of their
body?
Do people see the real you or do they judge you by your
face?
Do they stay long enough to hear your thoughts?
Or just long enough to hear the sound of your voice?
Do they have hearts of gold or cold souls?

Don't lose hope because of what these faceless people say.
Don't hold back on the things you do, look beyond the
sunset to find your love.
Don't hide from your future, do what it takes.
Love will look down deep to see the real you and won't care
how you look,
Just what you stand for.
You will know when the time is right in your heart,
Love's hard to find but if you try it will find you.

Ashleigh Robyn Corden

CONNECTION

Between oceans, there is land,
The past had brought us presence,
There is the rainforest and dry sand,
Crazy at times, we can lose the essence.

The valuable recognises loss,
Freedom makes us creators,
Inviting love is down to us,
Like good art draws spectators.

Your love for me is my bliss,
Sad moments are easier overcome,
The happiness I give you, you can cease,
There is plenty of joy for everyone.

A single mind full of love, is as strong,
When I can feel what you feel is good,
When sharing with others, you can't go wrong
And it's down to you my celebrating mood,
So thank you.

Beata Korabiowska

EMMA LAMBERT

Twenty-sixth of February 2008, a very sad day
It's the day Emma Lambert passed away

She'd been a good woman, helpful and caring
She would help those in need, she was thoughtful and
sharing
It hadn't been easy, she'd had a hard life
But she'd been a wonderful mother and a loyal wife

She always wanted to help others and become a nurse
But she put herself second and others first
She was kind to animals, she rescued a cat
Protected by the angels, said the badge on her hat

As she got older, her mobility became poor
But her stick and fluffy pink hat placed in readiness by the
door
She was ninety-two when she died
She'd worked so hard, now her body was worn out and
tired

It was today, Emma Lambert passed away
Twenty-sixth of February 2008, a very, very, sad day

June Lambert

MY HOLOCAUST NIGHTMARE

I live alone and have my share of nocturnal nightmare,
Last night I traversed the realms of the holocaust
massacre.
Across the sky flashed scenes from extermination camps,
Where six million Jews were killed, as averred by Adolf
Eichmann
By *Ghettoization*, open air shootings, gruesome camps,
Scenes of prisoners arriving by cattle train to extermination
camps,
Herded direct from platform to reception, naked, to gas
chambers.
Scenes of zyklon-B pellets being dropped into chambers
through vents,
Doors screwed shut, releasing toxic gas with murderous
intent,
Amidst shouting, screaming, victims perishing in torture,
Savagely removing gold fillings in their teeth with pliers,
Cutting women's' hair, bodies buried in pits covered with
lime, in tiers.
Scenes of naked children, victims of medical experiments.
Shivering, I woke up in a pool of sweat and panic
And my pressure in a galloping cystolic and diastolic,
Great, to my relief, it was only a horrendous nightmare,
De motuis nil nisi bonum, I breathed in prayer.

Welch Jeyaraj Balasingam

DOCKLAND NEW YEAR

It's midnight
Television sends synthetic cheer
But Dockland is quiet
Gone the sound of ships' sirens
Bringing in the year
The crews' *whoopee*, though lonely cry
Rockets cracking, flashing the sky
Men trying to unite with home by sound
The way lovers parted, dream the same moon

Strain the ear and if the wind is right
The sound of a now far distant boat
Kindles memories of yesteryear
The soul has gone from London's Dockland
On new year's night
But for those of us who knew, this as the only way of life
That memory cuts as deep, as a knife

Time, that master of all change
Has slowly gained its way
Now corporate palaces fill the sky
And sadly, the community has had its day

Bernard Tucker

YOUR MOTHER

She is always there to listen
To advise and hold your hand,
Sympathetic when your troubled
And will always understand.
There's a meal upon the table,
Your bed is nice and clean,
These jobs are done without a grudge
In the home she's always seen.
Show her respect; she's earned it,
Then tell her that you love her.
You only ever have one
It is of course your mother.

Vera Janczewski

I AM

I heard you calling me last night - I felt your fears.
Confused perspiration mixed with salted tears.
I reached for you, willing you to feel my warm embrace
Hoping through the midnight shadows you may see my
ghostly face.
Would I be how you'd imagined for we've never truly met?
Though I'm with you always, so your face I can't forget.
I'm with you in your waking hour until you go to bed.
I'm willing you to sleep at night and rest your weary head.
I'm with you in your haunted dreams - it's these I occupy.
I brush away the falling tears that you unknowingly cry.
I 'm in every drop of rain that falls, in every ray of sun.
I 'm within your sounds of laughter when I hear you having
fun.
I know your every hope and dream though I have only one.
My wish is I could find a voice so you can hear me call you,
Mum.

Sally Kemp

ON YARDLEY HILL

Every May, about this time,
My horse and I would make climb,
Along the forest paths until
We came at last, to Yardley Hill.

And up the narrow paths we'd race,
It was not I who set the pace.
We passed the bushes in a blur,
I needed neither whip nor spur.

And then, above the cobalt sky
The larks were shouting up on high
And always, everywhere we went
Arose the sweet, intoxicating scent

Of hawthorn bushes, pink and cream,
Like clouds of glory in a dream
And round about, in sprightly green,
The brave new leaves could all be seen.

We'd walk a while, then stop and stare
At beauty far beyond compare
And oh, my heart with joy would fill
To see the may on Yardley Hill.

Stella Redburn

OCEAN

Oh, how I love the pearlescent moon,
Hanging so bright, amid the black velvet night,
Beams on to the ocean,
Shimmers and gleams,
Those mystical caps,
Splash pebbles near me.
Salt lingers, in the cool summer air.
That brushes my face and tousles my hair,
And my sweetest love, of whom I adore,
I feel is beside me on those temperate shores,
Soon I shall turn and head home for my bed,
With the sounds of the ocean inside of my head.

Kim Moon

LONG AGO

Notting Hill was the place to be
With the blacksmith's forge at the top of the road
Children were happy you would see
Games galore came in cycles
Hopscotch, five stones, marbles and leapfrog.
There were street vendors that came 'round,
The baker, muffin man and Wall's ice cream trike
To name just three.
Charabanc outings to the country and parks,
Annual holidays by the sea.
In shops nearby butter was slapped into shape
With two wooden pats,
Sugar funnelled into a screw of blue paper.
The lamplighter came when twilight arrived
With his long pole to switch the lights on.
Sunday was special - a time for rest
Those were the days in my place of birth.

Lily Barnes

WORDS

These few words of purple prose,
Could never be lovelier than a rose,
Nor can this humble refrain,
Compare to bubbly pink champagne.

No matter how eloquent and intent,
Never as sweet as perfumed scent.
These words uttered 'neath a Bower,
Could ne'er be as beautiful as a flower.

Yet these words are all I have got,
To let you know you are in my heart.
Champagne and perfume I cannot afford
Only pen and paper mightier than the sword.

So take note, mark my word
Into a few lines, much can be read,
Champagne and perfume you may be fonder,
But these few lines of verse will last much longer.

James Sanderson

HOMEWARD BOUND

At last, the distant drone of engines,
Prime anxious eyes, to scan blackened skies.
Hands clasped to offer thanks to those heroes
Who have just penetrated night where the enemy lies.
The homeward flight of bomber command,
Marked by the Lancaster's powerful roar.
A mighty sound to those at home
Who witness the return of Blighty's shore.
Another sortie over, another mission run,
How many more to go before our aim is finally won?
England's hearts pounding, as aircraft salute the drome,
Once more we utter, *Well done boys, welcome home.*

Alan V Holton

THE PROSPECT OF RICHMOND

Human activity seen from a distance
Like waves on a far-off shore,
Slowed down, silenced, made archetypal.

A man sweeping leaves from a path
With the Thames bending behind him,
His thoughts invisible from this distance,
His feelings evaporating into sunlit mist.

A bus glides in the background,
Its cargo of frustrations
Smoothed into history.

Even I am a memory,
A sepia photo of one who once stood here,
Now largely forgotten.

Raymond Blake

GOLDFINCHES

With their crimson face and gold-barred wing
They're colourful and exotic too
I've never heard goldfinches sing
But they twitter as they flutter through

I saw a pair on our garden fence
When I was living at home as a child
I was struck by their magnificence
And thought they were cagebirds escaped to the wild

I've seen goldfinches on arable land
Out in the country near Sindlesham Mill
The sight would make me stop and stand
Their vivid plumage gave me such a thrill

I saw them last in the Isle of Wight
On a scrubby path, quite near to the sea
They gathered in the demi-light
Twittering animatedly

Valerie Luxton

DEPTH OF REALITY

Why do I feel so empty?
And feel that life has so little meaning now
I lost a precious gift not realising its value
Or the affect it had on my life.
Death, I know, is now the final goodbye,
Sudden, painful and so very sad.
Untimely, one may say, but inevitable
Although it still hurts me deep inside,
Why do I cry so often?
When in the past we argued so much
I wanted to be free from the suffocation
What I did not realise was that it was called love.
No matter how many times I wish
For you, and your love to return,
That what I want, cannot be returned to me
Something that is so hard to understand.
So here I stand in my new life
One I have to cope with and reason why
I try to make this new life work for me
When all I want to do is cry.

Julia McDougall

Dedicated to the memory of a loving husband and dad Ivan Ralph McDougall who left this life 14th December 2006.

HER OR ME?

She watches and anticipates
But what? She still does not know
Her sweat now trickling down her forehead, she wipes it
back just like her fears
Her tears are no longer welcome
She can see what was wrong but does not understand it
She can not understand it, time will not let her
The scars etched on her heart make it clear the turmoil
and pain is here to stay
She had forced the pain of yesterday on to tomorrow, and
she sits alone with tears she could not name
The brave ones have come back to haunt her
And all the past fears racing through her head, but too
hasty to sit and contemplate on at least one
Sorrow has become her master and she sits like a child
waiting to be told what to do
How to act, how to feel
A rollercoaster of differences, a hurricane of pain

But after the turmoil and confusion, there is only ever
silence

Jasmine Anthony

MISSING YOU

My heart feels like a weight of lead
The pain keeps going round in my head
The thought of not being with you again
Fills my whole body with such pain
I will never see your long, black hair
Nor see you sitting at the bottom of the stairs
Will never again hear you laugh
Or listen to you sing in the bath
Never hear you say, *Does my bum look big in this?*
And never again feel your kiss
Into your eyes, I will never again look
From now on, I'll just sit at home and read a book

Irene Chitty

HERE AND NOW

Chips hot from cone held in best friend's hands,
Estuary unfolds in neon sea and twilight sands.
Sky blushing at summer's touch, pull it tight,
Like a blanket. Pause and freeze-frame half light

And change channel. Tube pulls into platform eastbound,
Subterranean hair swept, mind gap. Pulsing electronic
sound,
Bodies crush, lights flash, bass beats brain like a drum,
Exchange loose change for latté, trust the end will never
come.

Outline these moments in eyeliner, laughing dreams that
weave
Through dances down pavements. Promises unbroken,
hype believed.

Josie Turner

104

ME

Lacking help, in terms of me
I can no longer be of aid to those who need me
Drink and smoke and stress and cards, items that exist
outside of me
I am the only one
I do not hold the power to change others
They exist in their worlds without me
I am only a player in the game of time
We play the cards, we drink the stuff, I even breathe the
smoke
I am not like them, I like to think
I have my own demons
I have myself
Myself to cope with
Friends who cannot take me
Take me for me
How am I to feel at ease?
Content is not a word I use
Not a word I know
Comfortable breaths and smiles of comfort
That is what I wish for
Meanwhile, I lie and wait for the time I can have myself
Myself to cope with

Lindsey Marks

POINTLESS

I saw you standing, waiting,
I saw you talking, hating
Someone. But you were alone
On that corner. A harsh moan,
For anyone and no-one,
Society is from whom you run.

People and places evolve,
How can we help to solve
Your mental pains disgrace?
How did you come to this place?
Devoid of all your worth,
Trampled, destroyed your mirth.

Live alone,
A cardboard home,
Take my pity
To your city,
Live out your days,
It's pointless anyway.

Charlotte Llewellyn

PASSING YEARS

Riding on a sea of time
Carried on waves of passing years
Walking through pages of life's ages
Changing with the tides of seasons
Tears like petals fall on blank pages
Smiles like fire's embers warm, welcoming
Melting anger like frost, fades slowly away
Laughter erupts like a volcano bubbling
Always, love stays as strong as a rock
Taking on countless shapes and faces
Sleep a welcoming call beckons closer
Nurturing, relaxing, embracing minds
Youth fades like blossom, gone in an instance
Spring passed, summer briefly ensues
Maturity an autumn of deep feelings
Winter approaches in dark, death-like shades
Riding nature's cycle of time
Facing human frailties, brittle emotions
A rainbow of life

Martine Gafney

SCENT OF RAIN

Drifting in a cold blanket that drapes the twilight
Passing fields, backyards, sleepy villages, green pastures;
Rows of lined up houses in bricks red and white
Silence infiltrated by, *anybody with tickets to Doncaster*

And sometimes of a train that zooms past with verve,
Crunchy crackle of crisps devoured till the last crumb;
A creaky seat back tray table that irks the nerve
Until scent of rain distances one from noise and senses
benumb.

Flying away to remember a land where mud was gently lift
By teasing winds just before the rain inspects its base;
Then comes beating down at the playful muddy drift
And that warm, glorious enchanting fragrance emanates.

But muddy land of the monsoon now miles away
Scent of rain persists, a different smell;
Unmatched in character, gloomy and grey
Wrapping this island eternally within its murky smell.

Bosky Nair

THE OAK SHEDS ITS SKIN

Shifting through this earth
I let myself be
Accepting my state and uncertainty

The limbs around are luscious
And something inside me feels - I - must -

Jump, thrust, climb
Dance, bounce, twine
Touch, caress and kiss these trembling
Sturdy trees

Bark in my nostrils
Against my cheeks, ivy leaves

Around me, spiders drift
Wings lift
Leaves mould
And the streams look on and laugh

Hannah Rose Tristram

Hannah Rose Tristram said: "I am a passionate singer and teacher of natural voice and songs. I play accordion and flute professionally and have a wealth of experience as an actor-musician. I care deeply about the environment and human equality and also love dancing, movement and yoga. My work grows from my experiences in the moment, my reflections on those and an enjoyment of different vocal sounds and rhythms. I would describe my style as honest, playful and direct. I am 22 and have an ambition to enable people to be expressive and to inspire inner-strength and integrity. My worst nightmare would be a world where there is no creativity, community or sharing. My website is www.naturalvoice.net/pages/hannah-rose.html"

DIFFERENT RACES

Us humans are all different,
We are all of a different race,
We have unique fingerprints,
All have a different face.

Black, white, Mexican people,
Chinese, Asian, Polish too,
But we are all human beings,
Just different, that's true.

All have different ways
Of living our lives each day.
Some believe in nothing at all,
Some believe to pray.

We all come from the same place,
We all have feelings so deep,
We all need food and water,
We all need to sleep.

Different races fight one another,
They forget we are all the same,
Only have different coloured skins,
Only have different names.

Marie Lambert

*Dedicated to the man who has made me realise what
happiness really is. Stephen, you know who you are.*

WHAT DISABILITIES?

The blind cannot see where they should walk,
But have the ability to listen and talk.

The deaf cannot hear but have their sight,
Their extra vigilance will see them right.

The mute cannot speak but can point, and mime;
To overcome obstacles they confront all the time.

The lame cannot walk, but with the use of a chair,
There's not much to stop them going anywhere.

The sick can be cured with medical aid;
The insecure and timid needn't be afraid.

The mentally ill have no visible sign;
Their heads in a turmoil most of the time.

People adapt to the conditions they suffer,
And offer support to one another.

There's none so resilient as a body that's hurt;
Their full emotions, they often assert.

The human body is so well created,
That disabilities seem over-rated.

Jim Bell

FRIENDSHIP

Kindness, patience and attention,
These three words we should employ.
Why is there lack of consideration,
Shown to pets we all enjoy?
Animals are much neglected,
Whether dog, horse, bird or cat.
Why keep pets if you can't cope?
With wars and hate we are unprotected,
And human beings can lose all hope.
God's creatures do deserve our duty,
They try to show us how they feel.
Some people help them all they can,
And cherish the beauty of our land.
So love and care should be a plus.
By holding out a helping hand,
Banish war, hate and ammunition,
Love your neighbour as yourself,
Remember that great old tradition,
So peace can reign with all of us.

Patricia Dunant

PEBBLE ON THE BEACH

Smoothed by the rhythms of vast waters
Stilled in the hold of the shore
Swept by timeless waves
Unmoved 'neath buoyant hulls
    sailing turquoise calm
Churned through mighty wash from
    monoliths of the sea
Hurled to deep dark streams
Spun in conflicting currents
Subsumed by tide's returning surges
Reclaimed in its sculptured dance
Beached.

Gillian Johnston

KALEIDOSCOPE

There's a kaleidoscope inside my head
When I close my eyes
With pictures that keep changing
Of every shape and size
Some are objects bright and gay
Others, faces that I don't know
Have these people belonged to me
From many years ago?
They all seem very happy
Blondes and brunettes too
That smile at me for a second
Then disappear from view
Life is like a kaleidoscope
All ups and downs and round and round
But when I open up my eyes
I'm firmly on the ground

Daphne Fryer

NATURE'S CHOIR

Red breasted minstrel
How gloriously you sing,
Proclaiming nature's beauty
As you fly upon the wing.

An orchestra of sounds
Echoes through the resonant trees,
It fills me with awe and wonder
When I feel nature's peaceful breeze.

It makes my heart glad
When I gaze upon the myriad trees,
I marvel at each intricate flower
And each designer leaf.

An eternal monument
To our Creator and King,
Nature's choir continues
To sing.

Charles Newburg

SUMMER

Lamb's tails hang on the silver birch,
A harbinger of spring,
Never mind the snowstorm,
Summer's a'cummin in.

Crocus and the snowdrop
And bluebells bravely ring,
The hailstones are pelting down,
But summer's a'cummin in.

Daisies push up through the grass,
Birds are on the wing,
Their tiny feet are frozen,
But summer's a'cummin in.

Soon all flowers will be blooming
And happily we'll sing,
The sun is shining down at last,
Now summer's a'cummin in.

Patricia Jerome

THE PARCEL

My lord, this is heavy, said mum as she struggled
Is it for me? said my big sister, Sam
Who's it for? John asked, whilst dropping his breakfast
Me! said the baby who slid in the jam
Dad tripped over the dog in all the commotion
And fell flat on his face in a heap on the floor
I just looked at the label and said
It's not for us
It belongs to the Martins who live next door

Nancy Burke

Dedicated to my darling dad Sidney George Gilbey who is always in our thoughts, forever in our hearts. We love and miss you.

ADRIFT ON THE SEA OF INGENUITY

Undoubted is his fascination with the language.
Like a cat this phenomenon is not to be tamed.
He is in love with her.
This consciousness among interwoven,
Mutually intelligible others.
They dance together like butterflies,
Devoted to the processes of transformation,
Revealed through the chemistry of the body.
Relayed by the seers,
Invited to the feast for the eyes,
The shore, the threshold
Between chaos and structure,
Is home to the organism,
A beserker who keeps a fertile silence,
Nesting in the jaws of the leviathan
At bay before death.

David Gavin

FOR JOHN

Could I dream to be the one you loved?
Great beauty, for which there are not enough pages.
Great peace, for which there are not enough prayers.
Rushing toward a torrent is born.
With this heart,
With this ring,

Me? You want me?
Her? She?
She who is nameless?
She who is faceless?
Can I bear to leave you? As I dare to stay.
Haunted that love will be stolen away.

To fall into the valleys and delve into the blue,
I study the shimmer and shift,
From pain, to joy, to tears,
I offer comfort for love and loss.
I have never loved like this before,
I swear to never again.
For whatever meek and lugubrious lies within,
My strength grows stronger as I let you in.

Natalie Clarke

A TOUCH OF SADNESS

What a powerful emotion is sadness, which can overwhelm
at times
For reasons which are unclear, leaving you feeling sad

What a shattering emotion is sadness, which can stop you
in your tracks
With a sudden force when the news is bad

What a draining emotion is sadness, which can take over
your life
Pushing all else into oblivion, exhausting your senses

What an essential emotion is sadness, which focuses the
mind
On the important things in life, breaking down fences

What an enlightening emotion is sadness, which puts
things into perspective
With unrelenting clarity, even when little can be done

What a transient emotion is sadness, which eventually
fades away
With the help of time, when the battle is finally won

Pauline Edwards

NO STEEPLEJACKS FOR ME

Do not send a steeplejack
To search my pinnacles of hope;
But rather let them stay
Virginal
Within the morning of my mind;

And as the skies
Grow misted with the heat of noon
I shall await
The twilight of remembering
And softly say:
It was the building
That caught the vital beams of day.

Mary Nugent

THE GIFT OF FRIENDSHIP

Friendship is a priceless gift,
It can't be bought or sold,
For its value is much greater,
Than mountains made of gold.
For gold is cold and lifeless,
It can neither see or hear
And in the times of trouble,
It is powerless to cheer,
It has no ears to listen,
No heart to understand.
It cannot bring you comfort,
Or reach out a helping hand.
So when you ask God for a gift,
Be thankful if he sends,
Not diamonds, pearls or riches.
But the gift of a good friend.

Janice Smith

SPRING

Daffodils dance,
Primroses hide
Under clean, green leaves.

Remember forget-me-nots,
Sky blue, background to
Bare branches, bursting with buds.

Birds nest, snails pest,
Hungry from hibernation,
Hedgehogs hunt.

Walls flower
And scent with hyacinths
The fresh, breezy air.

Sometimes
Sultry, soporific, somnolent storm
Clouds into throbbing, thunderous thrills.

So soon summer swelters.

Odette Buchanan

LENHAM REVISITED

Of cobbled stones and lime tree
A village that meant so much to me,
Those innocent happy, carefree days,
Time has changed in so many ways.

My father's once flourishing bakery
Is now the village library,
Those elegant tea rooms of bygone day
Have become a fast food take-away.

That little dingy sweet shop I knew so well
With its musty yet distinctive smell,
Where the aged proprietor dispensed homemade ice-cream
Has long departed the village scene.

Likewise my old school has suffered the same fate,
Demolished to accommodate a housing estate
And what of those old friends I once knew,
Burnt away as the early morning dew?

The friendly locals are still there;
The Red Lion and the Dog and Bear,
Still stands the church with its shining spire
Where I sang proudly in the choir.

Derek Weeks

MY CITY

The aroma of roasting coffee,
The smell of cigar smoke,
The whiteness of Finnish hills,
The darkness of burnt coke,
The bluntness of Abraham's knife,
The sharpness of an eye of a hawk.

Mischievous, snob, pretty, reckless,
Cruel on every admiring bloke,
She cuts the oceans up and down,
Fully dry, when everyone soak
My city is Gilgamesh's yearning,
Who chases it, reverts broke.

Hashim Salman

UNDERGROUND EYES

The tube, you know, is a funny thing,
Thousands of people pile right in.
You can stand or sit, next to thin or fat,
Crushed by a woman, or a man in a hat.
But what is nice, is catching an eye,
Of someone you like, and just as shy.
Both eyes meet, then away they'll look,
Diving down to a paper or book.
But seconds later, again they meet,
Their eyes collide in a welcoming greet.
Now it starts, the guessing and games,
What are the differences? What are the sames?
You can't help but smile, from inside a laugh,
Lucky today, they've crossed your path.
One last look before your station arrives,
Catching the romance of underground eyes.

Andrew Drury

NATURE

The day's almost over, the sun's nearly gone,
In the half light of evening life still goes on.
A fox runs by, eyes and ears all alert,
Tail streaming behind her, little face pert.
An owl hoots from the tree up above
And from somewhere there comes the call of a dove.
Rabbits playing, flicking their tails,
Hedgehogs hungrily searching for worms and snails.
Fireflies dancing, glowing so bright,
A vole dashes out, the owl has him in sight.
But the vole hears him coming and goes to ground.
A mole pops his head through the top of his hill,
He sniffs for danger, his body is still.
He decides it's not safe to venture outside;
He goes back to his tunnel where he can hide.
There by the stream something dark ran,
A pair of young otters are building a dam.
Night time now, the animals settle with a stretch and a yawn,
And sleep through the night 'til the breaking of dawn.

Patricia Maynard

THIS DOG'S NAME IS JACK

This dog's name is Jack
He was a lonely chap
He was abandoned
Left out to die
This dog's name is Jack
He was a lonely chap

Left in a field
Tied to a fence
Nobody to feed him
No means of escape
No comfort or care
Not when tied to a fence

Jack was dying
But look, who is this?
It was a kind old man
He took Jack home
He fed him and cared for him
He gave Jack a bone

This dog's name is Jack
Now he is a happy chap

Jennifer Bourne

THE LIGHTHOUSE

It must be wonderful to see a lighthouse shining
When you are at sea,
Because it looks very impressive and grand,
When you are on dry land.
It is truly a pleasing sight,
As it turns around its little light,
Keeping sailors safe in bad light and at night.
When the fog horn sounds,
We all hope nothing runs aground,
In this modern world, as things stand,
Satellite systems aren't so grand
And just a little, old lighthouse standing there,
So everyone can share,
I don't think it could be replaced,
What else could give you light in the right place?

David A Smith

Dedicated to my late mother and father, Maisie and Bill, for their inspiration through their love of verse.

CURTAINS AT A WINDOW

The little old lady stands behind the nets,
Feels old and alone, yet soon forgets.
Now she is spying on Betty across the way,
And the children excitedly at play.

It was not always as bad as this,
In her youth life was bliss.
However, in '39 she said farewell to her beau,
Looking through the window she watched him go.

Whilst watching through the panes of glass,
She saw Pete the postman walking upon the grass.
A telegram she noticed on top of sack,
Could it be news of her beau Jack?

It was a nice sunny day in '45,
She saw the postman, who said *he's alive*.
He had read the telegram he had brought today,
It's alright love, he's on his way.

Now once again she looks outside.
A soldier appears, her heart swells with pride;
It is her beau Jack. He has come to take her away,
He is taking her to heaven with him today.

Eileen Baldwin

Dedicated to darling Derek, our brave Lisa, family and friends, especially Sue Gorton, English tutor, and aunty Hilda. Thank you.

THE FIELDS WERE GREEN

The fields were green,
The trees were tall,
And birds were seen,
Now, where are they all?
The wind in the trees,
The blackbird's song,
The hum of the bees,
But where have they gone?
The golden corn
That reached the sky,
New creatures were born,
They've vanished, but why?

Men took their cranes and diggers there
And made the countryside look bare.
They laid their pipes and built their bricks
And no one seems to care.
The fields were green,
The trees were tall,
And no one seems to care.

Sharon Plumridge

Dedicated to my father Robert Ronald.

NET SHEDS PROTECT NETS

Between cliffs and marks of high tide
Net sheds survive three storeys high,
Wooden but tarred to prevent decay
They keep hemp and fishing nets dry.

All is safe for sheds and nets,
But the storms, the frets,
The unnatural high tides,
The moon's growing larger she cries,
Where is my John?
I know he'll come back
He'll soon sail home
But where is his smack?

Diana Godden

NEW DAY

Fragments of thought drift into consciousness
A half-forgotten dream, a haunting song,
A haze of bluebells in a wilderness
Not visited since childhood, long, so long
Since that mind-picture. Window-tapping rain
Insinuates, while gradually young light,
Muted and grey, reminds morning's domain;
Once more withdrawal of abandoned night.

The radio implodes with headline news.
Set conscientiously, insistent bleep
Of an alarm clock punctuates the views
Of broadcasters, listeners half-tuned to sleep.

A blackbird bravely heralds lessening rain,
Another day's potential still germane.

Beryl Cross

RAINBOW SOULS

Sights seen through clouded vision of rose,
As soft fingers trail down peach skin that glows.
Bringing to the blackness white light within,
Igniting red fire as love's show does begin.

Purple painted nails trace lines down his back,
The blues chased away by love that neither lack.
His hazel eyes a sharp contrast to her green,
The strings that tie their rainbow souls, unseen.

Kisses traced by pink lips slowly across her face,
A crimson blush soon takes over their place,
Neither rush as fingers run through brown hair,
They've all the time in the world, their love to share.

The black night breaks by the first ray,
Orange, golden sun, marking break of day.
Caresses slow over flushed, cooling skin,
The red fire of love continues to burn within.

Sleepy eyes slowly close out light of day,
Cuddled close, dreams sweep them away,
Their heads against soft pillows of peach,
Their souls of rainbow never out of reach.

Christine Ray

WILLOW BRANCHES

By the library, by the canal,
Stand two willow trees,
Bendy branches looking down.
Like cautious sisters at the church
Of watery wine. In the winter,
There are some yellows to dilute
The greens and brown,
As if they were an old print pad
That broke their colours on the trees,
Wavelets almost thinking,
Skating on sunlit triangles to re-tell
The eye world the wind has shaped.
These are their sums,
Like undone strings in tie,
That ravel themselves nicely,
Factors that divide the hairs,
The willow is unfurled
On a new and silken world.

I cannot see the things I see,
At least the way it seems to me.

Simon Partridge

*Dedicated to Geoffrey Partridge who said I might make a
good sailor. He is somewhere, looking out to sea.*

Simon Partridge said: "I love words and ideas and I have a
firm belief in the musical nature of English poetry. I learnt
to think from W H Auden at University where I expanded my
expressions into pure shape. I find old fashioned metre a
good back-drop. Can you sense the stilted pentameter in my
work? Other languages bear fruit; particularly useful is
Gerald Manley Hopkins' dissertation on Prosody, an
experimental overview. The work before you has simple
harmonies."

MY MAGIC GARDEN

In my magic garden there are blue harebells,
Lilies of the fields,
And poppies in profusion.

Fairies on dragon and damselflies,
Sail together side by side,
Over the meadows, under the trees,
In hushed and whispering near invisibility.

Green leprechaun in green, clover leaves,
Brush faerie dust o'er hearts on a sleeve,

And they dance on the midnight grass.

And the leaves on the trees,
Are rustled by the breeze,
Blowing in from the seas.

And michaelmas daisies and marigolds
Weave wandering feet to the paths in the grove.

Yonder is the rainbow,
Yonder it bends,
Wishing upon a star,
For the journey's end.

Lynn Tyler

SWEET CHERRIES

Sweet are the cherries,
That hang so delicately from their stem.
Round and robust,
Like your gaze, as it nurtures the wounds and tears of a
reckless world.
Glitter dances on my skin,
In my breath I am received and graced by your love,
Less restrained, without chains, we are free.
I will not forget thee, my love,
Our blissful adventures through our youth.
Through it all we have each other as the reflection of
gravity,
Yet I do not possess thee, that's why we are already in the
infinity of our affection.

Isabel Tepper

Born in London, **Isabel Tepper** has interests including
horse riding. "I started writing poetry when I was 12. I did
it for a school project and it just seemed to resonate within
my heart," she remarked. "My work is influenced by life
and all its gifts and I would describe my style as metaphys-
ical. I would like to be remembered as a poet who wrote
from the heart. I am a 29-year-old writer with an ambition
to earn enough to live a happy life." Isabel would like to be
God for a day and the person she would most like to meet
is the Dalai Lama. "I have written many poems and had
several published," added Isabel.

IT'S GOOD TO TALK

It's good to talk, or so they say,
Come sit with me, don't walk away,
I know you've had a difficult day,
But there's a bright, sunny sky beyond the grey.

We all have times when it's hard to cope,
You feel you're sliding down a slippery slope,
But for someone to listen can give you hope,
They'll build you a life raft and pull in the rope.

You can feel like you're in a deep dark hole,
You climb towards the light but back down you roll,
But bit by bit, with your heart and soul,
Set your sights on the prize and you'll achieve your goal.

It's not always easy to go it alone,
So to have someone to visit or be at the end of the phone
Can help lift your spirits, results have shown
And the seeds to recovery will then be sown.

Beverley R Stepney

THE KISS

Lips meeting, skin touching
Hearts racing, veins pulsing

Sound wanes, light fades
Time slows, space ends

Two mouths, one breath
Two hearts, one beat

Two minds, one thought
Two bodies, one soul

One

John Sephton

WHEN IT COUNTS

Recycling is something we all have to do
To keep our planet nice and blue.
So go on, give it a try,
It's easy to do and won't take long.
The melting of the arctic should make us think twice,
For some crazy reason,
No one seems to care
About pollution in the air.
All the risks that carbon monoxide leaves out there,
People of the world should beware.
The temperature of the sun will continue to rise
And the floods will increase and go sky high,
So do your bit for our planet,
Recycle your waste every day
And cut down on green housed gases,
When it counts and matters.

Linda Upfold

WAS IT WORTH IT?

Butter, tea, sugar, cheese;
These are some of the things,
I used to buy every week.
But no more.

In 2008 you are on rations again,
What you do is cut the items
In half and then again.
These have to last a month,
Or at least three weeks.

Instead of two cups of tea,
Only one.
But I will survive,
I wonder if you will.

Chocolate is a luxury now,
Pinch me, this is 2008 not 1938.
We went to war for six years,
To make a better life,
Was it worth it?
I think not.

Angela Dimond-Collins

LIFE

Way up high, in the passing skies,
There's a land that is full of dreams,
They swing, they sway, in the light of day,
They linger on the threads of moonbeams.

How often I have wished, that I could reach the skies,
And brush away with dreams, the tears from my eyes,
To banish from humanity, the wickedness and desires,
That smoulder like burning coals from the devil's fires.
To give back this world of shame, its tenderness and love,
Be rid of lies and blame and take the goodness from above.

How often I do seek sincerity and silence,
And meet people full inside, of misery and repentance,
Life is full of hopes and fears,
And through all the coming years,
The skies above with its land full of dreams, hopes and
fears,
Will always stay the same, through all the coming years.

Maria Keneta

FAIRY WOUND

Into the woods came the little people,
Sprites and fairies skipping along leafy trails.
And those of us who glimpsed midst hooded trees
Their filmy forms cried, *Look, look, see!*
Our senses touched, bewitched by magic veils,
Enchanted by the sun speckled summer's tease.

But the wood was felled and two hundred houses
Reared up in its place; trembling Aspens were replaced
With bricks and glass and yellow lines and cars,
Beer cans, empty cartons, a rusty door
And wheelie bins littered those once rambling paths.
So, the little people, homeless, came no more.

Jane L Willis

SONG FOUR

His eyes watch me,
Like a bluebird in the sky.

His mouth guides my wings,
He blows cool wind beneath my feet,
The smooth glided steps for my experiences.

His eyes are the beacon
Flight code of morals,
For freedoms beyond my limitations.

I know for sure He gives me love,
For my soul's been anchored in the Lord.

I feel the spirit. He reaches in my heart
And my heart inside this body.

Dorothy L McCuller

MY SILENT WORLD

As I walk the planet of life, a silent shadow follows in the
light,
I look around and down, to see if it grows,
Is it mine, or is it another's? I'd like to know.

My heart is pumping, my mind is racing, my hands are
shaking,
Who is that that follows? I don't know.
My eyes are scanning all around, with shadows following,
but no one I hear can be found.
The silence is painful, as there is no sound, as I continue
to walk around.
The pumping I hear is only from inside me,
As I walk this land with nobody beside me.

I see people's lips moving rapidly,
As they smile and laugh so funnily,
But I can only look on quietly,
With no words coming out, from inside me.

The shadow that follows me is mine.
My life is a world of silence, with only my hearing aid
buzzing lightly,
As I walk this life alone, silently.

Angela Jarrett

THE M4

Towards the west; towards the setting sun,
The endless streams of endless traffic run.
To steel and concrete, helpless Nature yields:
The M4's route carves through once silent fields;
Bisects a farmstead; blasts apart a hill;
Rips up and plunders ancient woods - and still
It bludgeons through the English countryside -
Once rich and green; now wrecked, undignified ...
What does a pretty landscape matter, though?
This is the age of cash and speed, you know.

A shameless, concrete, omnipresent scar;
A monument built to the motor car.

Dominic Newman

A HAT

A hat, a chapeau, a beret or toque
All have been worn by various folk.
A bowler, a homburg for the gent on the train,
To town every morning, his profits to gain.
The tubby, young school girl in Panama hat,
Her brother, just William, sporting his cap.
The years of the Charleston, when girls wore a cloche,
The caps of the soldiers fighting the Bosche.
Then Holmes, my dear Watson, the fussy, old talker,
His headgear of course was the famous deer stalker.
The stetson, fedora, sombrero and topper,
The helmet as worn by the neighbourhood copper.
Then Easter and chickens, time for a bonnet,
With flowers and lace and ribbons upon it.
The oft-mentioned saying, *I've got it off pat,*
To get well ahead you *must* get a hat.

D Maxfield

THE BRIDGE

One roof, two families, three individuals,
Each with unique feelings, needs, lives.
Daily they cross.

One bridge links two generations, three different back-
grounds,
Experiences, aspirations.
Daily they blend.

One elderly, two middle aged, three separate beings.
Nightly they unite.

The bridge's wobble and occasional creaks are detected by
the souls crossing
But the bridge doesn't always creak,
It can be as still as the waters beneath.
Sun shines on it
But the bridge can cast its shadow on the tranquil waters:
It expands and contracts according to the elements,
It will become weathered, rusty and old.
A new bridge will be needed ...
Until then

One roof, two families, three individuals,
Cross, blend and unite
On the bridge.

Carole Ann Herbert

HALFWAY BRAVE

From the workhouse to churchyard,
In almost one bound,
So many people and
Nary a sound.
It would take more than one drink,
To make *my* spirits rouse
Enough to live in *this*
Halfway house.
A name for your home?
Slab Happy, comes to mind,
Don't tell me,
You don't like it?
Well here's another,
Now please be fair,
How about,
The Mortician's lair?
You're such a sport
And took it all in good part,
But I think you should call your new home,
Bravehearts.

Diane Barham

*Dedicated to Diana Sands. The inspiration being her
proposed move into a converted "chapel of rest."*

Born in Kent, **Diane Barham** has interests including
reading, walking and theatre. "I started writing several
years ago because I enjoy it and my work is mainly aimed
at my family and friends," she remarked. "My work is
influenced by everyday life and I would describe my style as
fun and humorous." Aged 47, Diane is a pharmacy
assistant. "The person I would most like to meet is Pam
Ayres because I've always enjoyed her verses," added
Diane.

MOODS

Strange light, moonlight
Makes your dreams bright
Sad dawn, misty morn
Where have all your dreams gone?

Hot sun, blood runs
Enjoying all the fun
Cold blast, icicles fast
Good times never last

Light spring, birds sing
World of pretty things
Autumn hues sad news
All browns, no blues

Night falls, owl calls
Ink-black shawl
Day breaks, still lakes
Now come the heartaches

Margaret Lawrance

GUESS WHO

Now I see you, now I do not
You come and go from where to what
First in front and then behind
You're bigger too, but never mind
When days are bright, you're always there
I see you sitting in my chair
When days are dark, where do you go?
Oh eerie sister, I'll never know
You never come when snowflakes fall
When fire light glows, you're on my wall
Are you a better part of me?
A bigger heart, a smaller me,
My shadow

V L Fairall

CHRISTMAS MORN

The cold frost made the bushes shimmer
Set beneath the pale moon's glimmer
A cold wind caressed both hill and tarn
The sheep huddled closer in the barn
The children snuggling in their beds
Pulled the sheets around their heads
A bright star gleamed its heavenly glow
Shining on the Earth below
That same star shining let us know
That two thousand years ago
This same star shone on this abiding Earth
And told us of another birth
He came to us on that blessed day
To lead us all from harm's way
That blessed day that Christmas morn
When our Saviour baby boy was born

James Pyett

NIGHTINGALE

When we went wooing by the sea,
Leviathan came into view.
Did we stop wooing? No, not we.

When we a-wooing went, we knew
No fire or hurricane could
Prevent us when we meant to woo.

When we went wooing in the wood,
A nightingale began to sing,
More sweetly than an angel could,

And every creature in the ring
Of his enchantment held its tongue
And dared not move for listening

To notes so effortlessly flung,
We wondered how a mere bird could
Weave spells into the song he'd sung

So pure and powerful, we should
Forget what we had meant to do,
When we went wooing in the wood.

Charles Wright

FLIGHT PATH

And so it is within myself
That I must turn
Within myself that I may learn
Where I have gone.
I am lost.
I am free, somewhere, at what cost?
Was there anything before, I mean any more?
I am falling free, but, what is *me?*
Am I still a person, worsened
Or maybe a little chastened?
A little sobered, I drift on.
No flight path. No runway comes my way,
Where shall I land?

Wendy Gray

THE WATERMILL

Sitting back amongst the foothills,
By the sloping stream, a watermill,
The water churns the wheel around,
Then it gently cascades down,
Boulders, rocks and uneven ground,
While the wheat is finely ground,
The forest, all around, caresses,
The lone building like in an abyss,
The autumn colours, oh so vibrant,
Colour the gorge, nature's monument,
The squirrels go about their harvest,
Getting ready for their winters rest,
The birds calling o'er the air,
The mill still churns with great care,
Making flour for people to take,
Nature's gift, their bread to bake.

Sheree Stringer

OF THE ONE WITH FAR EYES

I sit across the sea, as if he were a friend,
Oblivious, those amongst us, we've solace each to lend.

I whisper of a love, with eyes deep as he,
A single glance could I behold the span, a century.

They lingered up the hills of Haydn, Chopin
And atop there, at Ellington, stared
Into euphonious land.

Tranquil eyes that gently danced to an endless symphony,
Waltzing through my narrow room,
Thought only promised me.

Oh I speak of one with far eyes, travelling endless miles
Encompassing all, big and small, of mere existence's trials.

Our far eyes met and in a blink, nevermore were we.
Still I reckon, in a split second, he made a vow to me.

Charcoal day befitting, tender words between,
I and sea, dear friend to me, let the gale intervene.

While lolling like a widow, though I may break or bend,
It aids to whisper of that lost love
With far eyes that never end.

Sheila Brown-Ellis

ROSES IN POLLYHAUGH

Across the field the gulls fly high,
The cows stand etched against the sky,
And now beneath the rising moon,
Poised in the dusk, the roses bloom,
Welcoming night with their perfume.

The moss rose through the apple tree;
Bends down its clustered heads to me,
Its day-pink turned to paper white,
In the embraces of the night.
Luminous in the dying light.

Against a wall, the thornless rose,
Redder and redder burns and glows.
Each flower a perfect entity,
Magic in its intensity,
The scent an ancient alchemy.

The garden now is cloaked in night,
A late bird calls on homeward flight,
Stirring the dark beneath the trees.
The roses sigh against a breeze,
Then all is still.

Gwen McIntyre

LIFE'S JOURNEY

Life is a journey,
Best travelled with a friend.
A strong shoulder to lean on,
As your weary way you wend.

A gentle hand to guide you,
To keep you going straight.
A wise head to urge caution,
When your heart says don't wait.

A soul mate to laugh with, not at you,
Someone to share your impossible dreams,
A tireless supporter,
Of all your hare-brained schemes.

Some people may never find,
Such a friend to share their life,
So I was truly blessed,
When my best friend asked me to be his wife.

Christine Collins

GUARDIAN ANGEL

Oh my guardian angel who watches over me day and night,
Be my inspiration and be my guiding light.

Protect me from evil and all the enemies that surround me
And may God's holy countenance be always upon thee.

Help me dearest Angel to be a better man,
To help others the best way that I can.

And bring me closer to Christ our lord
That I may do his will and inherit my reward.

Matthew Dodd

*Dedicated to my wonderful wife Martha who is the love of
my life and the inspiration of all I do.*

Born in Gravesend, **Matthew Dodd** has interests including
hiking, photography and playing the piano. "I started
writing a few years ago and I tend to write when I'm down
or if something in particular influences me," he
commented. "My work is influenced by family, religion and
my wife and I would describe my style as romantic and
serene. I would like to be remembered as a kind, honest
and loving person." Aged 25, Matthew is a postman with an
ambition to train to become a psychologist.

BLUEBELLS

The wood is such a pleasant bower
With sun dappling its shade,
And everywhere the scent and hue
Of bluebells, thickly laid.

As though a spirit of the wood
Has walked abroad at night,
And spread his magic, to create
A carpet, azure bright.

Perfection? Yes, for May, he feels,
But swiftly changes tune,
Cleansing out his palette
To hold new shades for June.

Sage, em'rald green he now employs.
Then autumn comes around,
When every leaf he daubs with gold
And wafts on to the ground.

And there each lies, quite dead, unmoved,
Upon the woodland floor,
'Til pushed aside by spears of green,
As bluebells grow once more.

Ann Pinder

I MISS YOU

I miss you now, come the night,
To have you near would feel so right,
Your warm embrace to hold me near,
Come the night, there is nothing to fear.

I miss you now, it's dark outside,
To ignore these feelings, I can't, I have tried.
The emptiness goes on and on,
Each day passes, I must be strong.

I miss you now, but come the day,
A call from you will come my way.
You will want to see me, a time, a place,
Then we will meet again, face to face.

Christine Kellett

LOVE THAT FINDS US

The love that finds us all is so well-known
The sun has risen and the birds have flown
It was that love with which the sun had shone
It is that love that lives within our bones
My love for her is never getting less
It lingers like the perfume on her dress
I begin to dream and not get stressed
She smiles away, and to me she's the best
The love we know comes unaware to us
We hasten it here so we run and rush
We feel close to each other, love can truss
And if it abruptly leaves, we feel crushed
The love we seek is so well-known all round
Still evasive and not easily found

Muhammad Khurram Salim

MITSUKAI

Cheer up, said the Mitsukai,
The Mitsukai with the thousand eyes

He covered me with vines,
Forest vines that entangle and intertwine,
Tying my skinny frame to his,
Crushing ribcage and mixing skin
Until we were neither man nor woman

One in a faded grey million

Our single, deformed body
Danced up into the sky,
Waltzing through mists
Of enchanting prose and foreign tongue

And looking back down
At the city below,
I wondered why I saw myself,
Myself before I had a twin,
Still sitting on the roof of a stranger's car,
Wishing us
A wonderful new life

Ryoko

GOLDEN EAGLE

My noble head was made from threads of gold
My beak from basalt and my claws from steel
My eyrie towers on a Highland crag
No human creature ventures where I reign

My piercing eyes survey all earthbound beasts
With icy scorn. They live or die by me
My lethal talons spare no trembling prey
On darkly looming wings, I swoop to kill

I soar above all trifling, earthly cares
The blueness of the sky rends as I glide
My sole companion the unbridled wind
The golden sun reflected in my crest

Turid Houston

ALONE

Far away from home, I stand here all alone
Wondering what I'm doing here, all alone
Each night I close my eyes and think
What if I die here all alone?
Beautiful as can be, the world around me
That I rather be with people around me
Uncertain times, I felt warmth and happiness
Yet in my heart as lonely as can be
And not knowing what life will be
Until I found what I have dreamed
Reassuring life will always bring happiness
And laughter it's what I've always dreamed
You never know what tomorrow will bring
So love the life you're in

Layka Ozkoc

THE LIGHT OF MY LIFE

By moss-banked paths under dappled trees,
Morning air is spiced with dew and May.
A white tail wags amidst bracken leaves,
His body alert, full of play.
Delight in movement, excitement at his walk,
Means running ahead at a sprightly pace,
With occasional stops to sniff and poke,
His curious nose into every place.

He lifts his head to imbibe the air,
Is that scent rabbit? Badger? Fox?
He smiles for a moment without a care,
Then off ahead he nimbly trots.
Loyalty and trust glow in his eyes,
He shares my every triumph and all my woes,
I love his warmth as he brushes my side,
And the way he speaks with a nudge from his nose.

But now he is gone, the light of my life.
He gave me the comfort of his caring heart,
He showed concern at my pain and strife,
And was my closest friend from the very start.

Pearl Davis

GYPSIES AND CHERRIES

So deep in garden forest a caravan lays,
Windows of laced drawn and bowl on ledge,
Cherries red so near a crystal ball.

Do we enter and pray for future told,
With old lady scarf in hair and grey,
Does she see and know, past worries and cares?

Bowl of cherries tempting,
Yet will only leave a stone, upturned and sticky,
Will she leave no dream untold?

Past the gated garden, way near dandelions,
Fly our silver six-pence into her hand,
Give me a bright reading, tell me fame will come.

Life a bowl of cherries, life full of stones,
Like the ones in graveyards, relatives know below,
Maybe gypsy lady, you can shine a light and tell.

Out with the fairies in my wildest dreams,
Like to sit with white lace on hand and red, green, gold,
Put my penny for thoughts with you and eat your cherries
too.

Alan Gardner

SILHOUETTES

The night sky red, silhouettes
the old pine standing alone on a barren hill.
Like a gladiator in all his glory
Bending its proud head to the evening breeze
Looking out across the land
Waiting.

Its tall frame carries the scars of old loves,
the hearts and names all belong to the past.
The lovers have grown old,
shrivelled and died.
But the old pine still stands
Looking out across the land
Waiting.

David Chierighini

Born in Mansfield, **David Chierighini** has interests
including watching football and racing. "I started writing in
my late 20's when my life slowed down and I started to
really feel alive," he commented. "My work is influenced by
my mother and I would describe my style as from-the-
heart. I would like to be remembered as a loving, caring
family man." Aged 60, David is married to Maureen and
has four children. "I have an ambition to be present at all
my grandchildren's weddings," added David.

FOOTPRINTS

For him, it has been an exhausting afternoon
Exploring the little bay;
Just like a young Robinson Crusoe
Without a Man Friday.

And his small footprints left in the sand
Fill by degrees with the lukewarm sea,
As he watches, mesmerised
Almost anaesthetised by the heat.

As his old green fishing net
Breaches the rock pool's outer calm,
It causes circles, concentrically formed,
Something like wrinkles on a once-perfect skin,

To grudgingly reveal, piecemeal
Treasures borrowed from the deep;
Red seaweed, pearlised shells
And a hermit crab that he cannot keep.

Well, maybe just for an hour or two.
Tell me - didn't you?

Jacqueline Cooke

IMAGININGS

Looking from my bedroom window
I see a wondrous sight,
And seem to feel my skin glow
With raptures of delight.
A wall of sparkling azure,
Gold palaces entice,
Green hills of gentle grandeur,
A glimpse of paradise,
With little red-roofed houses
To complete the fairy scene,
A place where beauty browses,
Is it really just a dream?
The wall blue paint and crumbled,
With bright graffiti crowned,
The hills, just rubbish tumbled
Across the barren ground.
Alas, my thoughts go wandering,
My brain leaks like a sieve,
My feeble mind keeps blundering
To my land of make believe.

Jack Scrafton

DREAM LOVER

The rising sun will never miss,
Shining on your elusive hair,
Laughing at me without a kiss,
As I am never there.

Do you know that my absent heart is,
Locked in a dream that passes by?
Being asleep, gone is the art,
To free my lonely sigh.

Stars embraced your natural birth,
Heaven has kissed your eyes above.
I wished you knew that here on earth,
How much, how much I love.

Alan Dickson

ONE ROSE, ALL FLOWERS

What can a poem about a rose convey
This harsh, hard third millennium, my dear?
Fragrance sweetening the fume-choked atmosphere?
Or scarlet in the city brown and grey?
Caring for Mother Earth, soft bloom to stay
Alive in parched, dry heat without a fear
Of global warming and the last nuclear
Explosion? Still the roses thrive today.

No. The strongest poetic rose unfolds
With all my heart in verse, longed-for lady:
Full-blooded deep from longing long for you.
Please be the gardener who in love beholds
Flowers - all kinds in poems abundantly
With scents to breathe and all colours in view.

Robert Duncan Martin

THE AVIATOR

I used to be an aviator
In a *kite* held together by string.
The wings were made of canvas
Sewn to a wood-framed skin.

The seats were made from sports cars
The propeller made from wood.
Cockpits were all open-air and
We flew as high as we could.

I dressed up like an aviator
In helmet, goggles and scarf.
I'd fly my plane in very high winds
And people below would laugh.

We only flew in daylight hours,
Not for over long,
As fuel was very precious,
But the planes were very strong.

We were the first real flyers
Of that we were so proud.
Now people use planes all the time
And travel in huge crowds.

Pat Sturgeon

VISION

I had a vision for twenty years I struggled: A list of things I
needed to do.

One day as I walked along the high street, I saw the sign
high up in the clouds, a message from heaven.

Pitman Training: a blue beacon beckoned me. I was
mesmerised; the vision I visualised was there for the
taking.

The hunger and thirst for knowledge gnawing deep inside
my soul.
Knowledge is power and no one can take that away from
you.

My vision to hold a certificate in my hand, so important,
that blue piece of paper.

A gateway to my dreams, this is where it all happens.
Your dreams, no longer pipe dreams can become reality,
If only you could believe in yourself.

You could be anything you want to be;
Sweat, toil and tears persevere and you will achieve.
The future is bright and beautiful,
Have faith: don't give up on yourself.

Sabiha Mertdogdu

DEAL - MY ADOPTED HOME

The golden pebbles crunch under my feet,
The tide drifts in like a transparent sheet,
The pier, what strength, what a sight,
People of all ages, fishing in earnest, *come on fish, bite.*

Tables and chairs, the pavements adorn,
The smell of fresh coffee and perhaps a cream horn.
My, this is stylish, what's missing? I know,
Youngsters watching a Punch and Judy show.

I stroll across the beach as boats unload their haul,
Cod, fresh herrings, we have 'e-mall.
The seagulls are circling and scream overhead,
Save some fresh fish for us, we prefer it to bread.

And just a little farther stands the castle bold,
Henry's defence against continentals, I'm told.
Deal's beauty and history oft' embrace me so,
Smugglers, military and miners tha' know.

Julius Caesar first came by this way, but unlike him, I'm
happy to stay.

Sheila Bamford

HARVEST TIME

Across the field, the harvest glides,
The farmer's inside it and joyously rides,
Down bends the corn as the breeze rustles through,
It's soon on our plates to feed me and you.

Red, orange and gold are the leaves on the ground,
Brown is the field mouse, so small and round.
Vaguely the scarecrow looks up to the sky,
Protecting the sweetcorn from the crow's prying eye.

A time for reaping, a time for giving,
A good time to think about all things living.
For looking back on the year so far,
And seeing how wonderful all nature's gifts are.

Ryan Smith

MORNING IN FEBRUARY

Outside my room, the early morning
Mist obscures the dull, damp
Courtyard.
Silently, it assumes its spectral
Shroud of white, covering and
Smothering all that stands
In its way.
All along the rooftops it
Creeps, ever advancing over
Waterlogged drains.
Moss-filled, winter-bare fences
Close ranks to shut out its
Intrepid advance, but to no avail,
Until the mid-morning sun repels
Winter's uninvited guest.

Richard J Scowen

THE BUS HOME

It's starting to rain as I stand in the queue;
There's only room for one or two.
It's full and I'm standing at the back
With school girls and boys and all their "tack".
Someone stood up and gave me their seat,
Just what was needed for my poor old feet.
The bus is definitely losing power,
The driver says nothing, and this is rush hour!
No doubt about it we've broken down
And that realisation raises a frown.
We just sit and wait and wait,
The driver says nothing and it's getting late.
Mums are called on mobile phones,
The young all wanting to get to their homes.
Forty minutes have passed us by,
The driver says nothing, not even a sigh.
No one complained or made a fuss,
Those of us left got off the bus.
But why oh why, when I went to town
Did the 401 have to go and break down?

Maureen Oakley

SEEING STARS

I can see a lot of stars,
They're right in front of me.
I don't need a telescope,
It's better than T.V.

They are all such lovely shades
Of purple, red and pink.
It's my own moving rainbow,
Which changes when I blink.

And I feel I'm floating,
Up somewhere really high,
Looking at the ground below
Like I've just learned to fly.

So how did I acquire this skill?
Has it been mine from birth?
Am I the only person who
Sees stars like these on earth?

Well, no, it's accidental,
My fault, my mistake.
Next time I'm in the garden,
I won't tread on the rake.

Iain McGrath

Born in Lincolnshire, **Iain McGrath** has interests including
amateur drama, sport, walking and writing. "I started
writing at school because I always enjoyed rhymes and doing
some drama encouraged me to write some songs," he
explained. "My work is influenced by politics, family and
chance encounters and I would describe my style as simple
and humorous. I would like to be remembered as a good
husband and father." Aged 51, Iain is married to Claire and
they have children James, Megan and Sarah.

WOMAN

The beauty of a woman lies in her heart.
The way she is never afraid
Of telling the truth,
About the passion that burns
In her soul.
She doesn't have to use an iron fist
To make her point known.
She carries new life and a new world inside
Her womb, aching to break free,
And choose a new path for history.
Woman protects us all,
As she gathers the world in her arms.
She encapsulates her love
Inside her touch and kiss or just a smile.

Lawrence Rich

LOSS

The cliffs are unfinished, an unpartnered dance
Caves are empty backsteps, disjointed as jazz
The land lurches with the wind on an offbeat
An improvisation, the counting all out
Letting the sea quietly fill the gaps
Only to emphasise the endless fractures
Where gulls litter the crevices, the clefts of their wings
Forming colons and commas, breaths, hesitations
A fumbling silence, an irregular rhythm
Of motion and pausing, again and again

So why have I come here to tie up loose ends?
As if the discord of the land, sea and air
Settled for a moment, and under the shore
A regular riff exists somewhere

Isabella Mead

THERE IS NOWHERE TO RUN

The ground is hard beneath calloused feet,
I reached the field to work the beet,
The sky is clear there is no sound,
Not even the birds to scratch the ground,
There is nowhere to run.

They come droning out of the sun,
I drop my machete and start to run,
The tall stem of the sugar beet,
Offers no protection from the enemy fleet,
There is nowhere to run.

Bullets spit across the parched ground,
Fear and confusion are all around,
I cower behind a broken stump,
And cover my ears as the bombs thump,
There is nowhere to run.

They've gone as quickly as they came,
The enemy has had its game,
The ground is hard beneath calloused feet,
As I return to work the beet,
There is nowhere to run.

May McLean

CHANGING SEASONS

These days, it's layers,
Hot and cold, all in an hour.
Animals, birds and humans bewildered,
The whole world confused,
As arctic winds provoke.
Weather patterns swirl around
And centuries of established life,
Ruthlessly ransacked by human raiders.
The circle of life rudely dislodged
And not for the first time,
Civilisation is perched on a slippery ledge,
And where is that precious ingredient,
Do you remember common sense?
Seasons and senses, singularly scuppered.

Margaret Ann Wheatley

WHO IS HE?

Who is this man showing me around this care home?
Does he have a girlfriend, or does he live alone?
If I get offered this job will I be working with him on his team?
If I'm offered this job but don't see him will I still be so keen?
His warm smile is so friendly like nothing I've seen before.
I swear I recognise him but I just can't be sure.
Why do I feel this instant connection between him and me?
Does it mean I'll be offered the job because it's meant to be?
What is this feeling I'm experiencing, my heart feels on fire?
Do I know him or is it purely the feeling of strong desire?
I do hope the manager phones me and says the job is mine.
If I'm working with this gorgeous man I'll manage just fine.

Louise Sarah Jones

HOOTS MON

One Sunday morning while you slept it off
I couldn't stand your sickly cough
Out to the garden I did go
And being a nosey so and so
I thought I heard a noise, a hoot
Was that an owl in hot pursuit?
I hooted back and stood to wait
Would my new friend take the bait?
I really was quite surprised
When *Owly* once again replied
And so it became a daily hack
To hoot at owl, and he'd hoot back.
This went on for many a day
Until my neighbour came to stay,
Her house backed onto the end of mine
With lots of trees where they entwined.
She said her husband was quite absurd
Because he would call to an owl he heard
And so we found out that there was no owl
Just me and him, friends not fowl.

Guy Aldridge

MOTOR CAR

My motor car is very nice
I drive with skill and ease
I do not say what I shall see
I go just where I please.

The other man on the other hand
Is such a frightful bore
He blocks my path and paps at me
Though for what I am not sure.

I of course have a perfect case
For some vague priority
A special skill, national need
An endangered minority?

I am taxed to think of a formulae
That will keep me worry free
Multipliers, escalators
Road tax and VAT.

The London rush is far too much
Don't come, stay away, no room
But if you do, I'll tax you too
Mr Livingston, I presume?

Andrew Hall

INSOMNIACS ANONYMOUS

It isn't fair, it shouldn't be,
I'm wide awake, it's half past three.
Insomnia is not a joke,
Besides me snores a happy bloke,
Tucked up inside the land of dreams.
He'll stay there snug all night. It seems
So wrong that he can sleep, while I
Am stuck here counting sheep. I sigh,
I twist and turn, then finally,
Get up and make a cup of tea.

Next night, awake, I ask, *What now?*
Will things improve, and if so, how?
A self-help group might do the trick,
That's it! I'm going to start one quick.
The sort that helps you to relax.
It will be called, *Insomniacs
Anonymous,* I'll be the chair,
I'll launch the group, we won't despair.
And when at last you've got it right,
I'll see you in my dreams. Goodnight.

Claire Wilson

Born in Sale, **Claire Wilson** has interests including
wandering in London without a map. "I started writing as a
teenager when I wrote about the teachers and I like to
entertain people," he remarked. "I am opportunistic and
like to capture occasions and I would describe my style as
lively and sometimes mildly disrespectful. I would like to be
remembered as a person who could encapsulate an
experience, event or person in a few words." Aged 65, Claire
is married to Robin and they have children Peter and Keith.

COLOUR-CODED WATERS

The sun is out
The sea is blue
When are you going to realise
I'm a much better angler than you?

The sun is out
Say the sea was grey
Your old fashioned fishing skills
Have had their day.

The sun is out
Pretend the sea was a dusty pink
Your crusty old multiplier
Belongs in a museum I think.

The sun is out
The sea has now ebbed
Park up one's boat
And stay in bed.

The sun is out
The sea's gone back to blue
And open your eyes
I'm so much better at fishing than you.

Robert Bergin

A WISH TO GRANT

Take my hand and follow me, I will share with you my
vision.
Ever hopeful you will see, there's a future for you and me.
When all our dreams come true, we'll walk hand in hand
together,
And maybe even have the will to last forever.

When you feel warm spirits surround your heart,
It's my silent way of saying, *I so dearly don't want to part.*
You've touched my world beyond belief, I feel warm and
safe it's true,
And I know however long I live, I'll always be here for you.

I met you in the darkness on a Sunday, late one eve,
I felt a strange kind of presence, which gave me a sense of
ease.
It's thanks to *Jiffy* our paths did cross, and I'll hold him
dear for that,
Maybe given the passage of time, You'll learn to love me
back.

God bless you Grant.

Diana Dooner

173

IANSFORD CASTLE

Nestling in the valley,
As the sun begins to rise,
Casting shadows through the remains
Of the now ruined castle.
Takes my mind to a place,
Far away in time
When our ancestors lived here,
Much harsher was the life then,
Than in today's peaceful backwater.
What battles or skirmishes
Could these ruins bear testimony,
To the suffering of our ancestors
Bourne bravery, so that we
Can today enjoy our liberty.

Ian Tudball

SHIPS ON THE THAMES

The wind does blow the ships to port,
Boats of many kinds:
Cruisers, yachts, containers too,
From many countries, not a few.
And tankers go to Canvey Isle,
Whilst old Thames barges
Race with style.
The tide is in,
The channel is deep,
But when 'tis out
The river sleeps.
When comes the dawn,
Ship-life is born,
On the estuary
And out to sea.

Nola Small

A NORMAL WORKING DAY

Thursday. A normal working day.
Did not know, for me, there would be no Friday.
Chatting helped my journey along,
A few minutes later, my young life gone.
Fanatical, evil or just insane.
Determined to kill or to maim.
Wedding planned for next year,
Now a funeral and many tears.
Survived, but grieving too,
Mourns, has one leg instead of two.
Briefcase found, an envelope sealed with a kiss,
The cards she'll receive read *sadly missed.*
Appointment arranged on her phone,
Her best friend will be dining alone.
This morning, his new baby cried,
Now his wife's crying, just heard he has died.
A mother frantically phoning, nearly insane,
Relief her daughter had missed that train.

Sylvia Adams

NATURE'S MUSIC

Music is like listening
To the wind.
Play it softly: it's like
A lullaby.
Play it loud: it takes you high
Into the sky,
Twirls you round
Like a leaf.
Music brings laughter,
Also sadness of past times,
Friendship and happiness
And love. For do we
Not love the wind,
When it's gentle and warm,
Whistling, then screeching
As it rushes round the tree tops,
Bringing thunder in its wake.
That is nature's music.

Rita White

BIRTHDAY

Another year gone, how time has flown
One year older and I still have a moan.
Reflecting upon years that are long past
I find recent ones moving too fast.
A wonderful life I've definitely had,
It's sad to hear of events that are really bad.
Life can be divided into different stages
So many things happen with all ages.
If I could choose one, which would it be?
Three years in Australia it has to be.
Meeting new people and teaching as well
Helped me to settle and really gel.
Working hard daily then home to play
Was always a perfect way to end a varied day.
Melbourne and Mount Isa was a dramatic drive
When life became so busy, as busy as a hive.
The four seasonal changes down in the south
Up to the heat left one dry in the mouth.
A house, a caravan and a pool thrown in
Was just so great for children and din.

Kirsten Hogben

Born in Asheridge, **Kirsten Hogben** has interests including
writing, reading and theatre-going. "I started writing in my
teens due to my love of books," she explained. "My work is
influenced by situations and my family and friends and I
would describe my style as off the cuff. I would like to be
remembered as someone who was friendly, caring and
sociable." Aged 64, Kirsten is a retired teacher and is
married to Peter. They have children Russell and David.
"The person I would most like to meet is Boris Johnson
because I found his TV programme so interesting and infor-
mative," added Kirsten.

SO NEAR TO THE END

I haven't been well now for quite some time,
So I thought I'd rest and make a rhyme.
I'm so very sad and all alone,
It's just so well I've got the phone,
I can talk to my friends, both near and far,
Also visit them in my little car.
My kids tell me that they love their mum,
But don't like seeing me looking so glum.
It's midnight now and time for bed,
I need to rest my weary head.
You never know, I just really might,
Sleep throughout all of the night.
But that doesn't happen to me, Kate,
I've never been able to sleep in late.
Tomorrow will be another day,
I'll try and stay happy, come what may.
I'll do nothing stupid, please do not fear,
'Cause I love you all, so very dear.

Kate Mackenzie

ORANGE TRACKS

Larch needles, plucked from the trees by last night's winds,
Blankets the tarmacadam and verges.
An orange, alien snow, with a single set of car tracks,
Central, moving with the contours of the road,
Until a disappearing bend removes them from sight.

Bracken, nettles and couch grass emerge from this unnat-
ural snow,
Beige, brown and lifeless.
Hornbeam, hawthorn, and beech, as a dysfunctional hedge,
Clinging to its leaves, produces a blaze of colour.
Accentuating a beautiful, lingering autumn,
Complementing the usual covering.

The larch woodland drifts into a chestnut coppice, bereft of
leaves,
Highlighted against an early morning blue sky,
Framed as a rare picture of autumn, for a selected few.

Jon Charge

MIRAGE

As a bird, fanned in petal talons, gracefully climbing into
the unknown, you fly.
From the grips of pristine passion, persistent and free, you
soar and glide away.
Ever nearer, always dancing, yet farther from a touch, so
profound.
Undulating stretch of desire, you create and disperse,
Your cheery claps vividly encompass the horizon.
Tinkered with melodic clamp, ever elusive, yet energising,
You roam around the skies, free, effervescent and splendid,
A serene epitome of beauty in sublime savour wrapped.
Free from fleeting grace, beautifully poised,
Gorgeously endowed with tact, beauty and elegance,
A sizzling fountain in time, sprinkled in soothing brilliance
With permanence and vigour profound;
Your person defined.
A true walking affection, a robust ardour you attract,
From the finest of minds, embedded in genuine want
Always ready to join your magnificent flight,
Beckoning with supreme, virgin desire, cuddled in subtle
ebullience,
Saying, *Come down little angel, roost with me.*

Regis O Nwofa

Regis O Nwofa said: "The power to express freely without
rigidly conforming to proper use of diction and grammatical
structure is what makes poetry unique. Having been
impeded with a stammer for many years, though I have
greatly overcome it now, I found poetry as an escape. It's a
form of self-unveiling, a freeing of my being and the best
channel to communicate those feelings and imaginations
that are difficult to convey conventionally. I love poetry and
see it as standing in the moment while bringing others to
share your thoughts and live in your own little world."

HEARTS

It is a pity when a pair of eyes can no longer
bare to acknowledge, a bustling, troubled world,
Cover them with your hands.
There is always then a chance you maybe just fine.
But ask yourself this question,
Are you giving up big time or small?
What is your choice?
Have you really lost all belief in the sun and the rain,
Feel indifferent that night always follows day,
And no longer care the world is rotating - whatever,
Or whether or not God really loves you?
But remember always, and remember hard, with hope,
You have a heart, it beats, it sings, it lives, it dances,
Listen to it this very second.
The heart is a store when the eyes cannot see and the
mind cannot think, a reserve for hopes and dreams.
There is a bonus, a wonderful one as hearts always heal,
Because they simply have to.

Beverley Harknett

PRIDE FEELS NO PAIN

Summer season in church, scantily dressed,
Cautiously, warmer jackets for all the rest.
You have your stoic presence to maintain,
And we know that pride feels no pain.

Giving another hairdo a whirl,
Rollers wound tightly for a sprightly curl,
Yet your complaining scalp you deny again,
Reinforcing that pride feels no pain.

Out for a trendy charity run,
Socks spurned, fashionably not done,
But through those blisters you boldly feign
To prove that pride feels no pain.

Betty Bukall

ONCE UPON A TOWN

London I loved when it was shabby and
Full of grace
People lived, loved and died there because
It was a place
Full of character and heart, though
Antique and perhaps staid
It drew you, held you. In it history
was made.
Now it's gone forever, in its place meets
the eye
Glass boxes with blank, windows, skyscrapers
towering high.
This is progress, so they say, we cannot be left behind,
Yet why do we lose so much on the way?
It's unbearably sad, I find.

Irene Bell

ON BALLETER HILL

The sky leans on the scraggy moor
Black as pitch and heavy with child
Rain grows pinprickly and bleakness blinks
Amongst the angry downpour - sudden
But not as relentless as the wind which hates

The ground; spongy, saturated
Gives way to rocks; gritty, immortal
All is darkened under the ultimate deluge
Then, faint white light on the horizon grows and glows
Sudden as it started, the bleeding sky's flow is stemmed as
it falters

A humble sun, dimmed by mists emerges
Shy, yet majestic
And with passionate intent, is soon fiercely intense
The sodden turfs
Hiss and sigh their surrender

Clare Gill

THE WIND FROM THE PAST

When the wind from the past is blowing
It will remind you of who you are
The hopes you had and values held,
Decisions made, paths you travelled
To arrive at where you are at
You'll see things you thought were gone
Forever from your mind
Places, faces, all you've done,
Good, bad, thoughtless, kind
Regrets and sorrows relived, times alone,
Memories to make you sad
But gratitude too for the love you've known,
Pleasures and joys you've had
For carefree days when you were young
And life was full and fair
The music you danced to and sung
Will rise and hang in the air
When the wind from the past is blowing

Marion Griffin

OLD AFRICA

From boy to man less trouble my growing
Under the blistering, boiling, Africa sun
Wide and wondrous childhood opening
As all days turned to fun
Farmyard and fields, orchards and space
And mountain, river and vlei
Horses, carts and cycles all race
No end to the doings of day and day
Special and spoilt in my halcyon time
No space for cares, whilst all sublime

And growing brought changes, but fun kept coming
My wondrous, tumultuous, young man memory
Spaces wide and wild for walking, climbing, hunting
This stretching farm with friends and privilege bounty
As caring and loyal and saintly the servants
As happy and cheerful, the brown-black workmen
Then workers sans schooling and prospects
No thought I for less privileged their condition
Doubts to surface at varsity and apartheid time
My advantaged position brought stark into line

Roland De La Harpe

SAFE IN THE HANDS OF JESUS

Safe in the hands of Jesus,
I am safe in the Lord.
Safe in the hands of Jesus,
As I trust in His word.

Safe from storm and tempest,
From within and from without,
Safe from every danger,
From the darts that fly about.

Safe from the world's temptations,
Safe in the narrow way,
Safe from sudden death,
When each night I kneel and pray.

Pray onto Christ my Saviour,
For so I've learnt to do.
You'll be safe in the hands of Jesus,
When you learn to pray to Him too.

Emmanuel Faithfulman

METAPHYSICAL

Metaphysical an outer-other-world weightless feeling
Suggests: man trying, dying to connect.
Dreaming, too esoteric to be scheming.
Earth by advanced aura ringed, somewhere
Out there, just maybe a clue to our future
When we too of a superior system maybe a part.
Reduced to a gas which into the cosmos will pass
Nothing remaining for today's egos sustaining.
Consumed, subsumed, presumed, assumed.
No vestiges remaining for exhuming.
Man and his dreams brought to naught,
When by evolution theory caught, and by
His priests taught, he was one of
God's own, especially chosen to die, then
Live with the Lord, His only Son in a mansion
With the room prepared, to be by angels shared
Adam and Eve, his wife granted eternal life.

Graham Watkins

Graham Watkins said: "I have interests including poetry, reading, photography and sports and I am a retired electrical engineer. I would describe my poetry style as discursive and wide ranging and I would like to be remembered as a good friend and an interesting, decent man. The person I would most like to meet is John Humphreys because I admire his incisive interviewing and sense of humour. To be Michael Palin for a world tour day would also be great."

TODAY'S PAPER

A cherry tree
With a labrador watering it
The golden liquid trickling down the bark
A Porsche Boxster with bloody seagulls shitting on it
Like a crazed ex ruining a wedding
A pond with a snake devouring the fish
A dislocated jaw sliding over an orange carp
A surfboard with a great white shark stalking beneath
Sharp teeth poised to sink into its prey
A council office with pigeons nesting in the old roof
Cooing and pooing down its Roman-esque architecture
A wooden floor with mites tunnelling their highways within
Weakening the aesthetics
A human with nature colliding

Christopher G Elliott

Born in Chichester, **Christopher G Elliott** has been writing
since 2001. "I started writing because I always had an
over-active imagination and have a love of literature," he
remarked. "My work is influenced by Christopher Reeve,
society and modern living and I would describe my style as
lucid, direct and observational. I would like to be
remembered as a good writer, poet and author, a dedicated
husband and father, as well as a caring person." Aged 30,
Christopher is a student with ambitions to work full-time
as a writer and to finish his degree. He is engaged to Amber
and they have one child, Maddison.

LITTLE BOY, LOST

The bitter disappointment upon waking
The harsh reality that you're not here
Re-live the pain of loss, refresh the grieving
After sleeping through the night with you so near

If only you could stay a little longer
Constant by my side throughout the day
To hold your face, to stroke your arm, your shoulder
To tell you all the things I didn't say

You hugged me and you kissed me and you told me
All the things you know I need to hear
But now I've got to face the bitter prospect
Of yet another day without you, dear

When I'm asleep, we always are together
We cling so tight, there is no letting go
No wonder I am always so damn tired
Tired of life without you? I'd say so

Linda Carrington

OLD FLAME

There she was on this fine night,
There she was, this bright light,
Standing there in blue and green,
Although they say it never should be seen.

She looked stunning, gorgeous and pretty,
I tried to speak, she smelt so sweet.
I managed to talk, little by little,
Until my jaw went brittle.

Her soft moist lips up against mine,
When they met my eyes did shine,
Bigger than ever before,
Holding her close for evermore.

Joe Creasey

WHETHER OR WEATHER

The weather governs what we do with our passing day,
Perhaps we plan to take a day to walk by the sea,
And we get up in the morning and it's raining heavily,
So we change our minds and think again.
It will have to be a trip to the cinema,
Or a visit to a portrait gallery.
It doesn't matter as long as we enjoy the company,
Of a friend or even a sibling and a great many more.
Just take the time to make sure,
So whether we stay at home or venture out,
If the weather is fine, we know what it's all about.
Still some of us like the rain and it doesn't stop us at all,
We will go and do anything, regards of the fall.
To end this poem, all I can say,
Is have a good time whatever the weather is today.

Iris Crew

LOVE COMES KNOCKING

There's a special kind of feeling when love knocks on your
door
It makes you feel so warm inside, not empty like before
It makes you smile throughout the day and stops you feel-
ing blue
It makes your heart just skip a beat when you know your
love is true
It makes the sun shine brighter when clouds are in the sky
It makes the day feel calmer when autumn winds blow high
It makes you shine with confidence as you crunch through
winter snow
And everyone will notice that you have a certain glow
It makes the birdsong louder as you wander through your
day
When springtime lifts your spirits, it makes you feel that
way
It makes you feel excitement as the days of summer start
When love comes knocking at your door and nestles in
your heart

Valerie Fry

DAFFODIL STILL

Daffodils now flutter
In the bitter easter wind
Buffeted by winter now
That follows in their spring

Spindrift flecks of blossom
Waves cast bough by creaking limb
Presaging the summer snow
The new ice age will bring

Autumn chords division
That tumescent distance haze
With insect bite insistence
Nags fullness to decay

Winter sun is shining
Brings another brighter day
By equinox and solstice
Rocked Gaia rules ok

Mark Shepherd

RESOURCEFUL PENS

I hold you in my hand each day
You let me work, you help me play.
You feel so smooth as my words you write
It's true what they say about a pen's might
With you in my hand I am witty and clever
My thoughts flow fast, drying up, never.
Your colours may change, your magic stays true
Oh resourceful pens, what am I without you?
A tale unfolds on a clean writing pad
A poem so happy or a story so sad.
A flight into fantasy, a journey so long,
Poetry of laughter, a veritable song.
A story that's spooky with a twist at the end
A long newsletter to be sent to a friend.
A few words in a card to say *How do you do?*
Oh resourceful pens, I'd be lost without you.

Pam Long

Born in Peacehaven, **Pam Long** has interests including
photography and writing. "I started writing about three
years ago after being in hospital for a long time," she
remarked. "My work is influenced by a mixture of life's
aspects and my style varies from humorous to serious. I
would like to be remembered for a sense of humour and my
depth of thought." Aged 60, Pam is retired with an
ambition to have her works published and remembered.
"The person I would most like to meet is Martina Cole
because she started off at zero and is now so well known,"
added Pam.

A TEAR FELL

God looked down with His all seeing eye
God looked down and gave a deep sigh
Just what on earth are they doing?
Plunging their globe into turmoil and ruin

Peace on earth was my belief
But man is causing too much grief
War and terror was not my invention
Sadly it seems their prime intention

They only want to bicker and fight
They never get their priorities right
Too much grasping and not enough giving
I don't like the way that man is living

It's time they got their act together
For I'm getting to the end of my tether
It's time I gave them a wake up call
To live in harmony one and all

God was feeling very let down
His face took on a fearsome frown
Why did I bother? Why did I try?
And a tear fell from His all seeing eye

Mark Randall

BUTTERFLY KISS

Soft as the down on a baby's head
Just like a whisper that's hardly been said
Flickering gently, a flame in a draft
Tinkling sound when my sweet mother laughed
How she would wake me, so close to my cheek
Quivering lashes so luscious and sleek

Watching the butterflies now I still miss
The tenderness there in her butterfly kiss

When I grew older I learned that I too
Could flutter my lashes and so awake you
With the slightest caress as my cheek brushed on yours
Like a breeze over mushrooms blows millions of spores
With the lightness of feathers that float on the air
It's the simplest way to show someone you care

So light is the touch, and the touch is so light
A butterfly kiss wins the gentleness fight

Jo Robson

NESSIE

Nessie, are you there in the dark and the deep,
Dreaming and waking in the depth of your loch?
You have been there so long, you must be asleep
Or do you pop up and get out and take stock?

A few years ago, by men you were seen.
At dead of night to their homes they were walking,
They told of your size and luminous skin
And their fright at the sight of you, stealthily stalking.

Nessie,
Don't be mean and stay down there,
We are in a bit of a state just up here,
So come up just this once and give us some cheer.

Jessie Luckhurst

GORMLEY IN LONDON

They balance London's skycape,
Teetering parapets, stargazing bridges,
Gazing the distant green perimeters,
Like stranded lighthouses, marooned, washed ashore,
Upright and still circling light.
Flash of inspiration, signal of humankind,
Breezing the sibilant shores of identity,
The diverse definition of habitation,
The toe-line of active regeneration,
The singular yet solitary solidarity.
A populace of expansive spatial aura,
Several hundred arm lengths of embrace
Or handshaking welcomes.
We crowd tube train, bus by day
And night-sleep a lighthouse.

Jacqueline Elson

DAUGHTERS

A daughter is a special gift,
Sent from up above,
Every day of your life,
To cherish and to love.

The love you bestow,
Upon her right from the start,
A true delight and joy,
Bringing a tingle to your heart.

A truly wondrous gift to receive,
Bringing you untold pleasure,
Every day brings a new memory,
For you to truly treasure.

It's not all sugar and spice,
Or all sweetness and light,
But one thing's for certain,
They set my world alight.

They are the blood,
That runs through my veins,
Every hour of every day,
My love for them remains.

Tracy Tabor

EVERY DAY

What will happen today, people will live, people will die
Some will laugh, some will cry,
People will walk, people will talk
Rivers run dry, birds fly high

Fields of green, fields of gold,
And as time goes by the world grows old
Sun, wind, and rain in all lands
It's all the same, there's wars that end peace,
From the North to the East

They say the world's a rainbow at the end where do we go?
For there's love and hate, and hate lives by the devil's gate
There's morning, noon and night, and ghost that walk after
light

There's right and wrong, good and bad, happy and sad
At the going down of the sun, a new born baby
Life has just begun, or a soul has passed away
This is what happens every day

Robert Lane

THE FINAL LEAF OF AUTUMN

In colours of turning twilight
I watched you hanging down
The final leaf of autumn
On a branch of golden brown

Through the seasons, your form did pass
From green to flames of rust
But, like most things once living
Your form will turn to dust

Then, as the wind was whining
You began your only fall
Past all those naked trees
That made you seem so small

It was in that magic moment
That I first did realise
All things are but one
No matter what the size

Martin Palin

I'M SORRY I WASN'T THERE

A silly disagreement
Being stubborn kept us apart
There is no blame to lay
On neither mine, nor your part

Too long did it go on for
It doesn't matter who was right
None of that's important
For nothing's black and white

Too late is it now
To agree to disagree
For the angels stopped you in your tracks
And set your spirit free

I wish we had more time
I hate how things turned out
But now you're in a better place
Of that I have no doubt

Now I'll never get the chance
To tell you I still care
To tell you that I'll miss you
And I'm sorry I wasn't there

Nikola Webb

A THING CALLED LOVE

Sometimes it's hard, when rain is pouring in.
I used to worry what tomorrow would bring.
Then you came along and changed my life around,
Gave me something to believe in, my life was upside down.
I used to have shut eyes and dream that it was true,
But now I don't, because I have the reality of you.
Some people ask me, *Are you making the right choice, is he
the one for you?*
And I do answer back truthfully, and that is, *Yes, yes I do.*
My life was an emotional rollercoaster, changed day by day,
But when you came into my life, my only emotion was
happiness, that's all I can say.
So now in my world, the sun can shine through,
So for that I say, *Thank you,* and, *I love you.*

Charlotte Louise Searle

THE AUCTIONEER

I contemplate. Nostalgia stands aghast.
The slog of ancient skill pervades this room.
Varnish and verdigris display the rheum
Of gaunt restorers, trying to make things last,
Which once were meant for those who lived too fast
And tripped. I'm here amid the gloom
Where a human night consumes Aladdin's tomb,
Bereft of candles, conjured from the past.

I grope and grope until new daylights dawn,
Which will not wash away this dust with rain.
No time warp makes craft seem less forlorn
Futility haunts my chill, unsubtle morn
For an affluent world will gnaw through all that's sane
While philosophy drip-feeds an idle brain.

Paul Jeffery

LULLABY FOR A BABY SEAL

Rocked by the billows, ocean your bed
Foam-crested pillows cradle your head
Winter chilled starlight frostily gleams
Spangled sky, snow bright, lighting your dreams

Little white daughter, peacefully sleep
Here in the water, close watch we'll keep
Wild winds with wintry moan soon will arise
Seal calf left all alone, no more lullabies

So sleep while you may, my flippers support you
At the end of the day, safe home I've brought you
Rest on the sand flecked with tide foam
Far from the land, soon you must roam

Learning to fish, keeping alive
Each baby seal, on its own, must survive
But when winter storms rage and wild is the water
My love will go with you, my little white daughter

Mavis Timms

GOODBYE TO THE SEA

Above the beach, the raucous gulls
Wheel and screech around the sky
A kindly pensioner with a bag of bread
Feeds them as they swoop on by.

Beneath them on the sea-washed sand
Lies the body of a herring gull all alone,
Motionless, one wing pointing skywards
Feathers ruffled, still windblown.

Waving a last farewell to the ocean,
No more to swoop above the sea,
No more to soar towards the heavens,
Unless, of course, its soul flies free.

Saturnine crows in mourning garb
Maintaining a noisy vigil,
Like pallbearers singing a doleful dirge
While the corpse lies quiet and still.

The incoming tide reclaims the gull,
Tossed from wave to wave,
Heading for its final resting place,
A turbulent, watery grave.

Colin Butler

LOST

Lost love, lost hearts, lost loved ones too,
Lost strength, lost hope, she feels dark and blue.
Lost luck, lost trust, the pain she feels,
Lost happiness, lost time, looking down at the pills.
Staring at the bottle, the pain wretched inside,
Everybody she loves has disowned her or died.
Picking up the bottle as she takes a deep breath,
All she wants now is death.
Lost pain, lost feelings; she's lost it all,
She feels no more, she cannot call.
Lost life, the bang on the door,
Too late, my friend. She feels no more.

Tolyna Read

Born in London, **Tolyna Read** has interests including poetry, animals, computers and acting. "I started writing when I wrote a poem as a birthday present for a friend," she explained. My work is influenced by my life and I would describe my style as rhyming. I would like to be remembered as a well-known writer." Aged 25, Tolyna is a housewife with an ambition to be an inspiration to others. "The person I would most like to meet is Dakota Fanning because I think she is amazing," added Tolyna.

JAMIE

I met my grandson yesterday
He's such a tiny gem
I've seen a lot of newborn babes
But he's not a bit like them
His features are so delicate
Thick hair all black and shiny
And ears and fingers just like ours
But oh so very tiny
I know he's not aware of me
Or of anything just yet
But I felt something between us
The first minute that we met
He looked at me directly
With his limpid dark brown eyes
And then he made some little sounds
Not normal babies' cries
His little arms stretched out to me
And then he gave a yawn
'Cause he's seen so many grown-ups
In the nine days he's been born
I told him we'd been best of friends
Until the day I died
He looked me up and down and then
That's when our Jamie cried

Chris Renham

THE STAGE OF LIFE

Life is a stage and I'm the principal character.
Playing a part,
Acting a role,
Trying to be someone else,
Hiding behind a mask.

As I hide true feelings,
Put up a front before the world,
My audience.
I'm fine,
Nothing's wrong,
I've not been crying.

Games of childhood become a way of life,
Imagination,
Make believe,
Just pretend.

What will I do when the mask slips,
And all is revealed?
The end of the play,
Cold slap of reality,
Time to accept myself.

Until then I continue my childish game,
Continue the act until the curtain falls.

Hannah Phaup

THE FLY

My children were playing in the garden
Whilst I was preparing tea
When I heard my twin daughter
Crying hysterically

I rushed quickly from the kitchen
To find out why she cries
She was holding out her finger
And on it was the smallest fly

My gosh, she was so panicked
And I was quite relieved
But am sorry to say
That laughter took over me

She kept looking at her finger
And then letting out a scream
My sides were aching
As I was bursting at the scene

I took hold of her finger
And blew the fly away
I scooped her in my arms
But all she wanted now
Was to go and play

Karen Cronin

CRYING CHILD

What would you say to a crying child?
Hold them tenderly, caress their brow?
Sing a lullaby to appease their mood?
Explain how sadness should leave them now,
Stop the sobbing before it reigns
And stays behind to pervert the brain?
Soothing words, spoken softly help
To return the mood to calmer thoughts.
The crying melt, silence returns,
Sleep will bring a welcome break
And forgotten, once awake again.
Replaced by sweeter dreams of life,
Parks and swings and endless play,
A new beginning on this brand new day.

Shirley Hannam

ACHIEVE

Under the grey matter is where it lives,
It shouldn't, I couldn't,
But It lays ever coiled,
Complete with a horrendous laugh,
Laughter that belongs only on
A ghost train ride.

The purpose,
To achieve, but never found,
Penultimate, out, out,
Down, down.
Further still,
Mind under matter,
Final want within a life's work,
A moment never, hopefully fully realised.

Melissa McGovern

MOTHERHOOD

Your heart stands still, your senses tingle,
Joy and wonder start to mingle.
Life on earth has just begun,
For your tiny baby son.

For a while you sit and stare,
Touch the golden downy hair.
Pat the hands that soon will start,
To tug the strings of your loving heart.

You count his chubby little toes,
Then his fingers, stroke his nose.
His tiny face, it seems to say,
I've just arrived, I'm here to stay.

Motherhood has just begun,
You've formed a bond now with your son,
In your gentle, tender way,
You'll guide his footsteps day by day.

Joy and tears will form a part,
Of his life right from the start,
But with your loving, helping hand,
He will take his place, become a man.

Valerie Helliar

TRUST

Do you trust a German soldier during the time of the war?
Or a criminal on the streets, breaking the government's
law?
Do you trust a drug, thinking that everything will be ok?
Thinking that one won't do any harm
But really, the drug is here to stay
Do you trust a stranger tracing your feet
Not realising they will be the last person you meet?
You do trust alcohol, do you?
Oh, it's only a laugh
The side effects take over, you've taken the wrong path
Do you trust an unknown driver
When you sit in the back of the car?
If only you could tell the future
The most terrifying disaster
The most painful scar
The world that you live in
Is not all fun and good
A weak mind, a weak heart
You now live in the wrong neighbourhood

Jessica Lempriere

SIX MEN AND A FLAG - IWO JIMA

I felt my boot claw at the rock - like a
Hungry tooth-filled mouth, a shark, or something
That consumed earth as though it were flesh.

The pole was cold from when we dropped it
In the sea, the flag was wet and slapped
Cool drops of saltwater onto our bristly faces.

We tore a track from the landing to the
Hill, kicking stones and volcanic glass
Into tunnels in the sand,
Grasping for handholds in the gun-thick air
We drove our point into the soil:
Six of America's children, beating off the wind.

Adham Smart

TO ONE WEARING THE VEIL

Blackout. I was appaled. The slitted eyes
like a bandit's cast in nefarious night
hiding some dark secret, a spy's,
a prisoner's brashly renouncing liberty,
snuffing out the suffragettes' fierce light,
while saying what about lascivious me?

Then reflection, my angel, ever wise,
to prevent my sympathies shuttering down,
by locking myself in a mental cell
with no advocacy but for the crown,
becomes my liberation, my inner voice,
that knows freedom's price only too well,
to be truly free we must have choice,
and in that choosing, we both walk free.

Wayne Carr

THE BLUETIT

There it lay
Fluffed up, frilled finery
Floating, floating
Brilliant blue, bursting
Into a body of brown
Breasted ochre
Faced down, facing death
In the guzzling gutters
Of that wet morning
Tiny, timorous tit trading
Songs with spring
What befell you?
What blow blighted
Your sonorous sonata?
Crushed your crescendoing
Cantata into the sucking sewers?
To fade into finality
To wet the windows
Of my soul

Aleene Hatchard

*Dedicated to my beloved husband David who gave me the
confidence and encouraged me in all aspects of my life.*

GREEN LADY WOOD

This curtained apron of the lady field,
Sitting sweet daisies of open yield,
Hair burnt orange, falling to green grass mosses,
She cries the song to the butterfly herders.
With strange, thick carols to imparting dense finch flocks,
Tapering tall towers of trees, nursing nature's charming
melodies.
Countless nodding bluebell blankets to pull me through
blue,
Charming quiet frivolities for the blinded shrew.
She is who whips those delicate pinched berries from elder
bushes,
And takes small, fine feathers for nesting nellies and tart
dandelion jellies.
Corn crust fields next to her blanketed dress,
Cutting off clear betwixt the royal empress and her falling
hair tresses.
Beneath her delicate petticoats are waking babies of giant
oaks,
Pressing to push the leaves from nestling lily white stoats,
Sleeping in the frosts from the winter slumber's deeds,
And waking with budded dew drops from crawling small
hedges and blankets of knotted reeds.
Closing herself dark at night and waking eyes fever at
dawn.
Rich supper thick mists lay at her bays and vanish into the
morn.

Clare Nightingale

PASSING OF TIME

When everything turns hazy with the passing of time,
Will I remember the look on your face, or even who you
were?
Will I remember my first ever skirt?
The day I left my mum and went down the road to school?

Will I remember my very first kiss?
The smell of your hair or the feel of your face?
How I thought I was so in love with you?

Will I remember the day that you left?
The torture and pain, torrents of abuse?
The feeling my heart had truly turned to stone?
Cold and angry and once again alone?

Will I remember through the haze of time?
Or will I sit in the sun, *tut* at the blackbird as he sings?
Or look through the rain and still see the dew?

Will I remember all wondrous things?
Sit with a look that's old and wise?
Or will I stare at the clouds?
Sit with anger and hate, as they darken my skies?

Angela Humphrey

DUCKS

Some, dipping, offer only tails to view;
One sleeps, her head laid neatly on her back.
Drakes preen and strut; ducks, chatting, softly quack.
There's humour, certainly, but there is too
A calm monotony in their refrain,
And watching them, we can philosophise:
Let fortunes change, let empires fall or rise,
Loves come and go, hearts break, the ducks remain.
And doubtless, looking down on this same green
Through drowsy centuries, the gods declare
That, bustling to those pointless private ends
With such absurd solemnity of air,
Along with charm and comedy, Man lends
A soothing changelessness to any scene.

Mary Hodgson

PATH TO THE SUN

A narrow path stretches itself full-length
To reach the western sky;
On either side, dark walls of close-knit shrubs
Press upward silently,
At path's end, a crimson ball of fire,
The slowly sinking sun,
Rosied by autumn mist.

Stillness, except for tiny silhouettes
Of distant wheeling gulls,
Weaving a pattern on the blood-red ball,
While softly splashing waves
Whisper a gentle lullaby of sound
To soothe the sleepy day
And usher in the night.

Beryl Chatfield

FALLING LEAVES

Wind travels through undergrowth so cruel,
As well as, indeed, fair pastures.
The mother cradles the baby, happiness aglow in her rosy
cheeks.
The wind passes through roses and other fine flora, too.
The infant begins its pursuit of life,
For spring is the beginning of beauty.

A cool breeze whets its diminishing power upon a leaf,
The leaf begins its descent, the child becomes an adult.
The heat heightens as the sun watches a young man's life
pass.
Man thinks he has a keen eye.
Yet he cannot see his fast approaching end,
For summer is the blind decline.

As summer ends, the trees cry,
As the man walks confidently on,
Trees cry their leaves away.
He loses faded memories,
For autumn is the failing hope.

Bare branches shed their colour,
Bare souls shed their life,
For winter is the end of beauty.

Ciaran McCormick

MAKE IT HAPPEN

It doesn't happen by itself
Life doesn't work that way,
If you want your heart's desire
You have to seize the day.

You have to be the midwife
To your fondly cherished dreams
As you breathe life into them
Rejoicing at their screams.

There's no fairy godmother
You make the luck you need,
Don't lose heart, but persevere,
In the end you will succeed.

Gillian Harris

HEALING GRACE

To be a nurse was my aim, hard work or so
It seemed at first, exhausted at the end
Of my first shift, I was glad when bedtime came.

At first, emotionally I felt drained while
Working on the ward when nursing the dying
And disabled as I felt their pain.

It was then that I took myself to task as this
Was their time of need, for them I had to be there,
to give them much needed loving, tender care.

When asked by a patient, *why wasn't I smiling?* I
Heard her say, *when you smile I know that I will have a
good day.*

Anne M Whitington

NOT THE DAWN CHORUS

At five o'clock, the show began,
Clouds overhead, moving, chasing,
Alternate grey shadows against the blue,
Swooping, diving, ducking, gliding,
A starling, multiplied a thousand fold.
Massed together for safety's sake,
Against the shore-based cliff marauders,
Sea pirates swooping from high overhead,
Single and squawking as seagulls wont,
Ever intent on sustenance.

Until the hoard began to dip,
Roosting and finding a niche to rest.
When the sun set, the air was quiet,
No insects remained, a fine starling feast.
Just the blazing white of the seagulls' throats,
Their flapping grey wings and their raucous croaks,
As they settled and squatted along the shore,
And peace reigned again over Eastbourne Pier.

Maureen Huitt

AFTERMATH

The way is clear throughout the road ahead,
The sweetish stench and clouds of war have flown.
A silence shrouds the erstwhile battle zone
As if to mourn the wreckage and the dead.
What was their home lies several miles beyond
And to the weary band of refugees,
Survivors of disaster and disease,
It sends a call to which they now respond.
They stumble on with hope and painful limbs,
The agony of exile starts to wane
When from across the bleak and shell scarred plain
They hear their city sounds as daylight dims.
The happiness of safe return implodes
As in their midst a cluster bomb explodes.

Rex Baker

ANYTHING FOR YOU

I'd give you my last rolo, I'd give you my last breath,
I'll stand by you forever and love you until my death.
I'd do anything for you, just say the word and it's done,
I'd sell my soul to please you, you're the love of my life, the one.
You could never ask too much of me,
No sacrifice is too great if it makes you happy.
I'd follow you through hell if I had to,
I'd go to the ends of the Earth with you.
I'd take your place on the green mile,
I'd go to any lengths to see you smile.
I love you more than you could ever know,
You're the light of the world, the star of the show.
You're the most incredible person I've ever met,
I owe you everything, I'm in your debt.

Nicki Watts

SEA LIFE

When lights dance over the island,
Like beautiful jewels in the dark,
And the castle clutches the dip in the hill,
That sweeps in from the lush country park.
When the crumbling vacant roofed tower,
Offers protection from a sea storm,
And a stiff daytime breeze makes kites set to flight,
Whilst the grass is still springy and warm.
When chimes from St Clements herald the day,
And summer catches the air,
Carrying scents of cockle shed life,
I wish I was once again there.
Back on the cliffs overlooking the Thames,
Watching the barges sail by,
In full sail for the regatta,
Beneath an uninterrupted blue sky.
This little town may be near a dead end,
That is known as Southend-on-Sea,
But I was born with salt in my blood,
And will always come back home to Leigh.

Sharon Forsdyke

WHERE DO BROWN CHERRY BLOSSOMS GO?

I want life to do with you, what the spring does with cherry
trees.
I want it to make you grow tall and proud and strong.
Then I want it to charm the best in you, out of you.
I want the whole world to see your blossoms.
I want them all to marvel at your greatness.

And after that glorious, kaleidoscope summer,
When the autumn comes, and all that is young and
beautiful and sublime must die,
I hope that she will come swiftly, that she will take you in
your sleep,
So that not even a surprised gasp escapes your soft lips.

So that you are taken in your prime.
So that no one can see you falter.
So that you do not see yourself falter.

I hope she takes you and wraps you safely in her cool
absoluteness,
As she takes you to wherever it is that brown cherry
blossoms go.

Chane Mackay

Born in South Africa, **Chane Mackay** has interests
including reading, writing, parties and exploring. "I started
writing because I love putting my thoughts and ideas onto
paper. The creative process excites me," he commented.
"My work is influenced by Jeanette Winterson and life in
general and I would describe my style as sensual, sombre
and colourful. I would like to be remembered as an
interesting and good-hearted woman of honour." Aged 19,
Chane is a student with ambitions to travel the world and
to find joy in all aspects of her life.

SERMON

Eyes straying wayward to the ceiling,
Voice raised high,
You leant upon the pulpit.
Robes askew and hastily swung,
The cross you carried slowly,
The air you breathed too deep.
You spoke of the breath
Of God before me,
And the wind that runneth through;
Of majesties.
Housman and D H Lawrence
Rang about the stone walls,
Crying, *Admit them, Admit them,*
To this unbeliever below.

Kim Sherwood

Welcome to the Short Story Society

Even if you have never had any prose published before, you should submit something to the Short Story Society. It's the perfect platform for your writing talents and gives you a fantastic opportunity to get your work published. Our aim is to help writers to create short stories and get them published and appreciated.

There's no membership fee to join the Society. To be a member you must submit a short story. If we do accept it, we will publish it in a compilation of short stories by other authors and give you five copies of the book. We will also put your story on our website at shortstorysociety.co.uk for visitors to read and enjoy - in the months leading up to the publication of the finished book.

"Having a short story published is a wonderful and inspirational learning process for all authors - especially those who have never had their prose published before," said Peter Quinn, Managing Director of United Press, publishers to the society.

Your next step is to submit a short story. It could be handwritten or it could be typewritten. It could be on e-mail or any kind of disc. You should send it to:
The Short Story Society
Admail 3735
London EC1B 1JB
www.shortstorysociety.co.uk
email - info@shortstorysociety.co.uk
phone - 0870 240 6190
fax - 0870 240 6191

Your story can be on any subject. It can be aimed at children, it can be a ghost story, it can be a love story, a horror story, a true life story.

£1,000 to the winner

All top poets never miss sending an annual entry for the National Poetry Anthology. Even if you have won through previously, and had your poetry published in it, this free competition is always open to you. And as it's the only big free poetry competition of its kind, it's the first one you should put on your list to submit your work to.

It's the biggest free annual poetry competition in the UK. Around 250 winners are selected every year, each one representing a different UK town. All winners are published in the National Poetry Anthology and all receive a free copy of the book. Many of these poets have never been published before. Send up to THREE poems (on any subject) up to 20 lines and 160 words each, by the annual closing date of **June 30th** to -

United Press Ltd
Admail 3735, London
EC1B 1JB
Tel 0870 240 6190
www.unitedpress.co.uk

One overall winner also receives a cheque for £1,000 and the National Poetry Champion Trophy.

Another £1,000 to be won

A poem about someone or something from your home town can win you a top prize in this annual competition. Anyone can submit up to three poems for the competition. The top poem will win £1,000 cash. There is no age limit and no entry fee. "The poem can be about something or someone from the poet's home area," explained United Press Publications Director, Peter Quinn. "It can be descriptive, historic, romantic, political, or personal - anything you like, as long as there is some local connection. This competition is open to anyone and is completely free to enter - so what have you got to lose?"

Send up to THREE poems, up to 20 lines and 160 words each, by the annual closing date of **December 31st** to the above address.